Brenda Poinsett

Why do I feel this way?

What every woman needs to know about depression

NAVPRESS

BRINGING TRUTH TO LIFE
NavPress Publishing Group
P.O. Box 35001, Colorado Springs, Colorado 80935

The Navigators is an international Christian organization. Our mission is to reach, disciple, and equip people to know Christ and to make Him known through successive generations. We envision multitudes of diverse people in the United States and every other nation who have a passionate love for Christ, live a lifestyle of sharing Christ's love, and multiply spiritual laborers among those without Christ.

NavPress is the publishing ministry of The Navigators. NavPress publications help believers learn biblical truth and apply what they learn to their lives and ministries. Our mission is to stimulate spiritual formation among our readers.

© 1996 by Brenda Poinsett
All rights reserved. No part of this publication may be reproduced in any form without written
    permission from NavPress, P.O. Box 35001, Colorado Springs, CO 80935.
Library of Congress Catalog Card Number: 96-13119
ISBN 08910-99247

Cover photograph: Photodisk

Unless otherwise identified, all Scripture quotations in this publication are taken from the HOLY BIBLE: NEW INTERNATIONAL VERSION ® (NIV®). Copyright © 1973, 1978, 1984 by International Bible Society. Used by permission of Zondervan Publishing House. All rights reserved. Other versions used include: *The Living Bible* (TLB), © 1971 owned by assignment by the Illinois Regional Bank N.A. (as trustee), used by permission of Tyndale House Publishers, Inc., Wheaton, IL 60189; the *Good News Bible: Today's English Version* (TEV), copyright © American Bible Society 1966, 1971, 1976; the *New King James Version* (NKJV), copyright © 1979, 1980, 1982, 1990, Thomas Nelson Inc., Publishers; and the *King James Version*.

Poinsett, Brenda.
        Why do I feel this way? : what every woman needs to know about depression /
Brenda Poinsett.
        p.   cm.
        Includes bibliographical references.
        ISBN 0-89109-924-7 (paper)
        1. Depression, Mental—Popular works.   2. Women—Mental health.
3. Depression, Mental—Religious aspects—Christianity.   I. Title.
RC537.P65   1996
616.85'27'0082—dc20   96-13119
                                                                                                 CIP

Printed in the United States of America

1 2 3 4 5 6 7 8 9 10 11 12 13 14 15 / 00 99 98 97 96

Contents

To Marilyn

"Silver and gold have I none;
but such as I have give I thee:
In the name of Jesus. . . ."
ACTS 3:6 (KJV)

Foreword

Once in a while a book is written that speaks to a need neglected for too long a time. *Why Do I Feel This Way?* is such a resource. It has been worth the wait. Perhaps one of the best statements to make about this book is twofold: It is comprehensive, but also very readable.

What is said is blended with insight to the extent that a reader might say, "This author really knows what she is talking about," and that is true! By the time you finish reading you will know more than you ever expected. The author weaves together medical, psychological, and biblical insights in a skillful manner. The purpose of the book is apparent: to accurately inform, to give practical help to handle depression, and finally to build a healthier lifestyle.

This is a book for men and women, as well as for professionals and nonprofessionals. This work will be welcomed and widely used.

—H. NORMAN WRIGHT

Acknowledgments

Encouragement is very important to a writer. I'm grateful for the encouragement many people offered in the way of interest and promised prayers as I worked on this book. Norman Wright's encouragement got this book started. He recognized the need for a book on depression for Christian women, written by a woman. Wright and Sally Wofford Girand offered advice on presenting the idea to publishers. That's how I met Liz Heaney, senior editorial consultant at NavPress. She shared Wright's concern for women and spearheaded the book's development.

A writer is always concerned with writing clearly and accurately. I appreciate those at NavPress who edited the manuscript. I also appreciate the help of those who read the manuscript to check for clarity and accuracy: Juliet Matthews, M.A., Clinic Therapist, Depression Treatment Clinic, South Central Mental Health Centers, Inc., Bloomington, Indiana; Allen Zehr, ACSW, Bedford Regional Medical Center, Bedford, Indiana; Cathleen Ingle of Cambridge House, Muncie, Indiana; and Anna Ruth Young, Oakland City University, Bedford, Indiana.

Jerry Hughes, librarian at Oakland City University-Bedford, was supportive with enthusiasm, resources, and encouraging words from the time the book contract was signed. The librarians of Bedford's public library were also helpful in obtaining resources for me through interlibrary loan. Some Bedford pharmacists supplied information about antidepressants, but they preferred not to be listed by name in the acknowledgments.

Many friends were supportive. In particular, I would like to mention

Kay Dawson, Martene Smith, Susan Miller, Peggy Brooks, and Judy Hickman. Kay sent resources my way. Martene did some phone research for me in the early days of the writing. Susan and Peggy prayed for me through the writing process. Judy provided a wonderful Thanksgiving meal to give me extra writing time during my Thanksgiving break from teaching.

My sons, Jim, Joel, and Ben, encouraged me through questions like, "How's the book going?" and "What are you working on now?"

My husband, Bob, has been my sounding board as I sorted through the information and differing opinions of experts about depression. Long ago I nicknamed Bob "Barnabas" after the Barnabas in the book of Acts. Like that Barnabas, who was given the name because he was an encourager, Bob is a person of encouragement, and I thank him along with the others listed here.

Besides the encouragers, I want to thank friends and acquaintances who have allowed me to write about portions of their struggle with depression. These people are nameless or are mentioned by another name within the manuscript. The details of their circumstances have been altered to protect their identities. I appreciate the struggle they have experienced, and I appreciate their willingness to reveal their stories to the readers of this book.

PART ONE

WHAT IS DEPRESSION?

Chapter One

Knowing Makes All the Difference

The next time you have lunch with three female friends, think about this: One of you will be seriously depressed at some point in life. The next time you are at a family reunion, mentally divide the women present into groups of four. Look at your group—perhaps your mother, a sister, an aunt, you. One of you will be seriously depressed at some point in life. The next time you are in a Bible study group, look at the women participants. One out of every four will suffer a serious depression at some time.

Depression is clutching women as never before. Dr. Ellen McGrath, who chaired the American Psychological Association national task force on women and depression, writes, "It's estimated that at least one of every four women in America will suffer from a serious depression in her lifetime."[1] That estimate does not include the number of women who will experience milder depressions.

It hasn't always been this way. According to Dr. Marty Seligman, a leading depression expert at the University of Pennsylvania, today's women are estimated to suffer from depression ten times more often than their grandmothers.[2] Younger women seem to be at an even higher risk for depression. "Their suicide rate has skyrocketed 300 percent in the past twenty years, and it's now estimated that nearly one out of every three women eighteen to twenty-four is significantly depressed."[3]

Depression has become a mental health epidemic among women. One way or another, every woman's life will be touched by depression. Either she or a woman she knows will suffer from this illness. That's why we all need to know about it.

KNOWLEDGE BRINGS POWER

Jesus said that knowing the truth sets a person free (John 8:32). He was referring to knowing Him in order to be set free from the power of sin, but His words have wider application. Knowledge frees. Knowledge about depression can release a depressed person from depression's crippling grip and give those who aren't depressed the tools for helping those who are.

Knowledge provides understanding and a label for what ails us— we know what we are fighting. With knowledge also comes control— we don't have to be helpless victims.

Many people who don't understand the illness use the word *depression* as a vague catch-all term. Before I became knowledgeable about depression, I said things like, "I'm depressed" or "It's so depressing" to cover a variety of feelings. I used the words lightly to indicate any passing mood or negative feeling, what we call the blahs, the blues. When I felt distraught, frustrated, or tired, I said I was depressed. When I needed a haircut or had car trouble, I felt depressed. I've since learned that depression can encompass all these things and more. Depression can be a mood, a symptom of an illness, or an illness in itself.

THE BLAHS

When we don't feel good about life and we are down on ourselves, we are depressed. Many things can affect our mood: emotional or physical stress, lack of sleep, the weather, the time of year (such as Christmas or spring), our country's political climate, and a host of other things.

These moods fluctuate in intensity and length, depending on the conditions involved. When we get our hair cut, when the car gets repaired, or when Christmas is over, we feel better. At one point our mood was depressed, but now the mood has passed.

A SYMPTOM OF PHYSICAL PROBLEMS

We may feel depressed when something is physically wrong. Depressive feelings may accompany a physical illness or disorder, such as a viral illness or even a minor infection. Body disorders that list depression as a symptom include ulcers, rheumatoid arthritis, hypoglycemia, hypothyroidism, and fatigue. When the physical problem clears up or is under control, we no longer feel depressed.

Depression may also emerge as a side effect of some medications. High blood pressure medicines, birth control pills, and steroids, such as cortisone and prednisone, may cause depression in some people. The same low kind of feelings described as a depressive mood may be present and persist for a longer time. When the drug or medication is discontinued, the depressive feelings go away.

WHEN DEPRESSION IS AN ILLNESS

The illness of depression is where the one-woman-in-four statistic applies. This is a disorder that includes both physical and psychological symptoms. It is more severe and longer lasting than a low mood. When depression is an illness, the low mood persists. It doesn't leave when Christmas is over or the physical difficulty clears up. It makes itself at home and permeates a woman's being. She loses her ability to cope with life and manage her day-to-day experiences.

Depressed people often talk about "not caring any more." They might say something like, "I feel as if I'm in the bottom of a well and can't get out" or "I feel like I'm in a tunnel and there's no light at the end." Life becomes a continual struggle characterized by sadness and despair.

Depression robs us of vigor and hope. The usually well-groomed woman starts to look unkempt. The once-talkative woman becomes silent and withdrawn. The good cook loses weight, noticeably so. When friends ask about her dieting secret, she shrugs her shoulders and says, "I just don't feel like eating."

These changes linger; a loss of interest in conversation or food may continue for months. And there may be other changes in sleeping patterns or sexual desire. Self-confidence drops as the depressed woman sees no way out. But like other illnesses, depression does have identifiable symptoms and methods of treatment. There *is* a way out. This book is about how to find that way.

HELPING OURSELVES

In the planning stage of this book, I asked a question of a woman who had experienced recurring episodes of depression: "What one question would you like answered in a book on depression?"

She answered, "Why do I feel this way?"

I'm with her. I've always wanted to know why I feel the way I do. That's why, when I learned I was depressed and not just feeling blue, I began research on my illness. What I learned helped me deal with the depression and my moods. I gained freedom to be the person God designed me to be and to experience the abundant life Jesus promised. My freedom didn't come without struggle, but it wouldn't have been possible at all without knowledge. Learning about depression was the beginning of my way out.

Part of helping ourselves is knowing what we're up against. Depression is not a simple illness; it can't be easily traced and treated like a germ with an antibiotic. The symptoms of the illness may vary from individual to individual and recurring bouts of depression may vary with the same person. Some people are more predisposed to depression than others. Even experts disagree over the causes and the cures of depression. The best thing a woman can do for herself is to become her own mental health advocate.

When we know the symptoms of depression, the forms it takes and what triggers it, we improve our self-awareness and become more skilled at recognizing when something feels wrong. When we know how to get over depression and how to build resistance to it, we improve our chances of avoiding this insidious illness.

HELPING OTHERS

Our knowledge about depression can also be used to help others. Linda began to cry when I asked her why she'd missed an assignment. That's not typical behavior for a college student. The other students looked away and some shuffled their notes. *Maybe Linda is very shy or tears up easily,* I thought. *From now on, I'll have to talk to this sensitive student in private.*

After class, Linda tried to explain why she missed the assignment.

She cried again and sighed heavily as if she were carrying the weight of the world on her shoulders. When I explained the consequences of the missed assignment, she couldn't follow what I was saying.

The third time Linda cried in my presence, she said, "I'm sorry for my behavior. I don't know why I'm like this. I don't understand why I keep crying."

"You mean this isn't your normal behavior?"

"No, and I don't know what's wrong with me."

Considering her symptoms—unusual bouts of crying, lack of concentration, a heavy weighed-down feeling—I wondered if she could be depressed. I told Linda I wanted to bring her something to read—a book I had written called *Understanding A Woman's Depression*. The next time she came to class, relief shone from her eyes. She wasn't free from her symptoms, but now she understood why she felt so sad. It had a name: depression. Linda had a lot of work to do to get completely well, but knowing what was wrong was the big first step toward that goal.

Depression affects us, our friends, our daughters, our mothers, our sisters, our coworkers, and our fellow church members. Understanding what depression is and how it manifests itself will help us help ourselves and will enable us to empathize with, encourage, and support women who become depressed.

We need a concerned, informed sisterhood to help each other gain freedom from depression's strong hold. I can't form a sisterhood alone, but through this book I can offer information on depression as a first step in helping ourselves and those around us. Knowledge is the place to start.

Chapter Two

All Women Are Not Equal

I was so encouraged by the knowledge I gained when I researched depression that I wanted to tell other women. One Sunday morning I announced, "At our next class meeting, let's talk about depression." Twenty-nine women showed up—the highest attendance ever. After I talked about a book on depression, I shared some of my personal struggles with the illness. My honesty unleashed confessions from many others. In fact, interest ran so high that we continued our "war stories" over cake and coffee.

The youngest woman in the group had stayed unusually quiet. She finally said, "I appreciate what you women are saying, but I haven't the foggiest idea what you are talking about. I've never experienced anything like what you're describing." The rest of us responded in chorus, "You will, dear, you will."

No one is immune from depression. No one is exempt from life's stresses. Sooner or later, all of us experience events that can trigger depression—lost jobs, failed relationships, broken promises, deep disappointments.

CHRISTIANS CAN BE DEPRESSED

I asked a Christian woman in her seventies if she had ever been depressed. "No," she replied. "How could you be a person of faith and be depressed? Those are contradictory terms." Many Christians share this opinion. But it simply isn't true. One only has to look at Scripture to see that some notable people of faith struggled with depression. Jeremiah was called the weeping prophet. "Oh, that my eyes were a fountain of tears; I would weep forever . . ." (9:1, TLB). Excessive weeping is associated with depression, and so is exaggeration of one's condition. Jeremiah said, "Desperate is my wound. My grief is great. My sickness is incurable, but I must bear it" (10:19, TLB).

The writer of Psalms 42 and 43 was depressed. He had been removed from the Jerusalem temple, a place where he went faithfully to worship God. Describing himself as "cast down," the psalmist confessed to God his feelings of despondency and asked for strength.

Four Old Testament giants wanted to die, a symptom of severe depression. Moses asked God to kill him (Numbers 11:14-15). He felt his responsibilities were too much. (Many women could identify with Moses' complaint!) The accumulation of the Israelites' complaints wearied and discouraged Moses, and he wanted out.

In a single day, Job lost everything—possessions, servants, family. Then followed prolonged physical suffering that shook Job's faith to the core. He wished he'd never been born; he wanted the peace and release of death. After Elijah's victorious stand against Baal, he fled from the wrath of Queen Jezebel and asked God to take his life (1 Kings 19:4). Jonah, too, despaired and wanted to die. He was upset because God canceled His plans to destroy Nineveh; he wanted God to confine His love and mercy to Israel.

Depression does not represent moral weakness or personal failure. Both Elijah and Jonah wanted to die after a spiritual high point in their lives! Moses was an extraordinary leader. Jeremiah was a long-suffering spokesperson for God; and Job made that wonderful proclamation, "I know that my Redeemer lives" (19:25, NKJV).

Clearly, anyone—including people of faith—can become depressed. But not everyone suffers debilitating depression. Research has shown that some people are predisposed to depression.

AM I AT RISK?

Several risk factors raise a woman's vulnerability to depression. I'll introduce them briefly here and discuss them more specifically in later chapters.

A family history of depression. According to Dr. Donald F. Klein and Dr. Paul H. Wender, "The brothers, sisters, parents, and children of a depressed person have a risk of approximately 20 to 25 percent of having the disease themselves. This contrasts sharply with the brothers and sisters, parents and children of a nondepressed person, 5 to 6 percent of whom may have the disorder."[1]

Perhaps a particular gene is passed on from one generation to the next or certain thought and response patterns are learned from one's family. In other words, an inherited risk factor for depression could have biological origins or environmental origins or a combination of both.

Chemical imbalance. Predisposition toward depression could be due to imbalances of certain mood-regulating neurotransmitters in the brain. Neurotransmitters are chemical messengers that transmit electrochemical signals between brain cells. According to an article in *American Health,* "Levels of the neurotransmitters may be abnormally low, or the neural receptors that normally intercept neurotransmitters as they pass from cell to cell may malfunction."[2]

Genetics could cause the chemical imbalance, or life experiences might create changes in the central nervous system that alter neurochemistry. This alteration places a person at higher risk for depression.

Personality type. People who have a negative view of life—pessimistic, brooding, and critical of themselves and others—are prone to depression. "They see the world as cruel and unsupportive, themselves as unworthy and the future as hopeless."[3]

Experiences in early life. "Painful experiences in early life can sow the seeds of future gloom."[4] Childhood sexual abuse or the loss of a parent increases a woman's risk for depression as an adult.

Gender. Statistics indicate that women may be more prone to depression than men.

+ For every male diagnosed as having depression, there are generally two or more women.
+ After puberty, women show more depression than men.
+ Women in all walks of life are more likely to be depressed than men, although research suggests that depression is most likely to be found at both ends of the economic spectrum. It is more prevalent in professional women and in

those with low income, as well as in those with little personal support and in substance abusers.[5]

Some experts blame women's higher depression rate on the fact that women seek professional help more readily than men do. Susan Nolen-Hoeksema, a Stanford University researcher, disagrees. In her book, *Sex Differences in Depression*, she critically evaluated the evidence for each theory on why women are more prone to depression than men. She cited ten studies that failed to find support for the hypothesis that women's greater tendency toward depression is because they are more willing to report being depressed than men. She summarizes that men's unwillingness to admit their depressive symptoms has not been consistently supported. "Men appear to be just as likely to admit and seek help for a given level of depression, suggesting that the higher rates of depression in women are not merely the result of men's underreporting of depressive symptoms."[6] Women really do get depressed at a higher rate.

We don't like the idea that women are more predisposed to depression than men. As one woman told me, "Predisposition sounds like predestination. The risk factors make it sound like some people are doomed to be depressed. I don't like the sound of that; I like to think I have more power than that over my life."

The good news is that women *do* have considerable power over their lives.

AWARENESS MEANS POWER

Predisposition to depression does not dictate a lack of personal power. Neither does it imply inferiority; females do not possess a defective gene that causes depression.

Predisposition doesn't even mean that a person will become depressed. "Even if an illness is genetic, that does not mean other factors do not play a role in its development."[7] Depression is mysterious. Some people with high-risk profiles never get depressed. Some people with no known risk factors do get depressed. Predisposition is not a jail sentence. However, life is full of losses and disappointments that can trigger depression. If a woman understands that she is vulnerable to depression, she can learn to spot depressive triggers and possibly avoid them or at least diminish their power. If a woman acknowledges her vulnerability, she can learn how to be an effective gardener of her inner soil. Awareness can lead to preventing depressive seeds from taking root and growing into dominating plants. No woman has to be doomed to a life of depression. However, all women are not equal when it comes to facing life's difficulties. An attitude from other women that sends the message, "If I can do it, if I can face 'X' problem without going under, so can you," is not only destructive and judgmental, it is rooted in ignorance. It just isn't so.

This is good news for those who are burdened with depression. And for those who have escaped depression's dark cloud, it should be an impetus for a compassionate attitude toward others.

Chapter Three

Recognizing the Clues

~

"Is it all right to pray for affirmation of one's salvation?" she asked. I was talking with a woman at a singles' retreat where I was a speaker. I started to answer her question with a quick yes when I noticed her eyes were filled with tears. Instead I replied, "Tell me what you are experiencing." Mindy said she no longer felt like she was a Christian. She had been praying for God's reassurance for several months but there had been no change.

Her tears prompted me to say, "Has this question affected your sleeping?"

"Yes, I've been awakening early in the morning and can't get back to sleep. If God would just reassure me, I know I could sleep better."

"How is your appetite?"

Mindy glared at me as if to say, "What's food got to do with it?" then said, "Food doesn't interest me right now."

Within a few minutes, she had revealed four symptoms associated with depression: tears, difficulty sleeping, loss of appetite, and a need for reassurance. Many other symptoms are associated with depression, and they are not necessarily listed in diagnostic manuals or medical journals. One psychiatrist I know asks his patients if there are cobwebs in the house. "If patients aren't bathing," he says, "if their house isn't clean, if they can't get out of bed—those are signs that they're depressed."

Symptoms offer us clues. They can help us spot depression in ourselves or others. Symptoms vary from individual to individual and may vary with the same person in recurring depressive episodes. But there are some classic symptoms:

1. *Feeling sad.* You appear dejected and discouraged. You think of yourself as feeling blue or down in the dumps. Facial expressions reveal your state of mind—a drooping mouth, downcast eyes, a wrinkled brow. You feel listless and you look tired and strained.

2. *Loss of interest in life.* You experience a sharp decrease in your ability to feel pleasure. You've lost interest in things you used to enjoy—career, hobbies, mission activities, family and friends. You begin to approach life in a passive mode and don't care if anything gets done.

Everyone feels sad or disinterested in life at times, but in a truly depressed person the feelings persist. If sadness or loss of pleasure persist for more than two weeks *and* if you develop three or more of the following symptoms, you may be depressed.

3. *Disturbed sleeping patterns.* The most common physical symptom of depression is a marked change in sleeping patterns—snapping awake in the middle of the night for no apparent reason, waking early in the morning and not being able to go back to sleep, not being able to fall asleep, or sleeping too often or for too long a period. Even the quality of sleep is different. You awaken easily and respond to small noises that wouldn't disturb the nondepressed sleeper.

4. *Abnormalities in appetite.* Usually your appetite decreases and you lose weight. However, your appetite may increase, and you may overeat or binge compulsively.

5. *Change in sexual desire.* You find sex less interesting and pleasurable. Your capacity for orgasm may diminish. Your menstrual cycle may become irregular or stop altogether.

While most depressed women report a decreased interest in sex, others report a heightened interest and become sexually indiscriminate.

6. *Feeling tired all the time.* You feel exhausted or fatigued for no reason. Any woman is bound to feel tired, even for several days at a time, but she'll usually know why. The depressed woman feels tired but doesn't know why.

7. *Trouble concentrating, thinking, remembering, or deciding.* You lose your capacity for clear thinking; you feel fuzzyheaded or muddled. You may have trouble putting things people say or do into proper perspective. It's hard to concentrate enough to read, listen to others talk, or

make a decision. Sometimes even simple decisions are difficult, such as what clothes to put on in the morning or what to feed the children for breakfast. And no matter what you decide it always seems wrong.

8. *Feelings of agitation or retardation.* Agitation is increased nervous activity, such as pacing and hand-wringing or constantly moving about. In depression, agitation is characterized by restlessness, pacing, and repetitive speech. Retardation is motionless apathy. You feel unusually slowed down, as if it's too much trouble to move about and you're dragging heavy weights everywhere you go.

9. *Feelings of irritability and resentment.* You feel an unusual amount of anger and resentment, and this contributes to your irritability. External pressures and responsibilities seem overwhelming. You get angry at the people who keep asking you to do things but you're afraid to show your anger. *What if I explode, clobber someone, or go to pieces?* you wonder. You're tied in knots over the struggle. Not being able to do anything about it, you hold on to the anger.

10. *Feelings of discouragement and pessimism.* Pessimism or extreme discouragement in a normally positive person is a sign of depression. You may become petulant and distrustful or absorbed with melancholic topics. You'll take the gloomiest view possible of your situation. If you try to do something about it, any trifling annoyance will discourage you.

11. *Feeling worthless or guilty.* You have a negative self-concept, express strong self-disapproval, and feel worthless.

You are your own worst critic; you blame yourself for everything. You feel guilty because you're not living up to others' expectations or your own. You take responsibility for acts and events that, realistically, are outside of your control. You magnify wrongs and feel guilty out of proportion to the act. "It rained at the picnic and it's all my fault."

12. *Feelings of inadequacy.* It's as though you suddenly think you're much less attractive or competent than you had previously thought. You view yourself as deficient in qualities that are important to you, such as appearance, intelligence, spiritual maturity, or your ability to manage your children.

13. *Brooding about the past.* "My heart breaks when I remember the past," says the psalmist (42:4, TEV). The depressed woman is very introspective. You're preoccupied with recurring morbid thoughts. The same images keep jamming your thoughts again and again. Your preoccupa-

tion is excessive. You go over and over all kinds of wrongs in the past, both real and imagined.

14. *Crying more than usual.* "Day and night I cry, and tears are my only food" (Psalm 42:3, TEV). You have an involuntary tendency to cry—you cry often or feel like crying often—and you may have an increased intensity in tears if you already cry easily. Those who rarely cry may suddenly start crying for reasons that never used to bother them.

15. *Feeling extremely needy.* You feel deprived of emotional support and crave affection and reassurance from others. You may long for your husband or friends to notice how miserable you are and come to your rescue, yet you act as if you don't need anyone. You withdraw from social activities and stay near home.

Christian women may feel an estrangement from God during their depressions even as they feel a desperate need for His help. One woman told me, "I desperately wanted Jesus to reach out in love and touch me." Some depressed Christians, like Mindy, may doubt if they were ever saved. Others may wonder if the Holy Spirit is ever going to work in their lives again.

16. *Suffering from physical complaints with no medical explanation.* You suffer from diarrhea or, more frequently, constipation. You complain of severe headaches, backaches, tightness in the head, heaviness in the chest, tingling in the limbs, rapid heartbeat, and heart palpitations. Sometimes these physical symptoms cause women and their doctors to focus on the physical complaints and miss the depression altogether.

17. *Increased use of alcohol.* You begin to use alcohol as an attempt to relieve your despair or to feel better, or you increase your alcohol consumption.

18. *Feelings of hopelessness.* Just as a cough is a symptom of pneumonia, hopelessness is a symptom of depression. You feel that nothing will ever go right again. You feel trapped by the circumstances that brought on your depression and can see no way out. Even when the situation is not hopeless, you *feel* that it is.

19. *Recurrent thoughts of death or suicide.* If hopelessness lingers, you may develop a heightened awareness of the absurdity of life and wonder if there's any point in going on. Death preoccupies your thoughts and appears preferable to living. Suicide looks, at times, like

the only way to rid yourself of intolerable tension.

20. *Delusions and hallucinations.* Delusions are false beliefs that are rigidly held, even in the face of strong evidence to the contrary. For example, you may be convinced you committed a crime when you didn't or that you are poor when you aren't. Hallucinations are perceptions for which there is no external cause. Usually the hallucination is something the depressed person hears or sees but occasionally can involve experiences of taste, touch, or smell.[1] Delusions and hallucinations indicate that you have lost contact with reality. *If you are thinking about suicide, having delusional thoughts, or hallucinating, go to a hospital emergency room or call a crisis line right now.*

If we recognize the clues for depression, we can ask for help. Many people don't get the help they need because they don't spot the clues. Learning the associated symptoms of depression gives us the recognition advantage. When I recognized Mindy might be depressed, I didn't immediately blurt it out. The more we talked, though, the more I was convinced, so I tactfully suggested she might be depressed. She adamantly insisted she was not. I pointed out the symptoms I observed, but she still resisted.

I didn't press the issue; I could have been wrong. Our conversation did prompt Mindy to see a doctor after she returned home. He confirmed she was depressed and she began treatment. When she was well, Mindy wrote to say she no longer worried about her salvation. When her depression ended, so did her doubts.

Chapter Four

Unmasking the Faces of Depression

～

After the publication of my first book on depression, as I was waiting to give a talk on the subject, I watched the women entering the room and noticed one woman whose countenance was grayish and sad. She walked slowly, as if every step took great effort. *Now there's a depressed woman,* I thought, *if I ever saw one.*

During my talk I listed the twenty symptoms of depression. When I asked if anyone had a question, this woman raised her hand. She said, "I don't understand. I have all the symptoms except I don't use alcohol and I don't hallucinate, but I am not depressed."

I thought she was probably in denial and I rephrased her comment. "You have most of the symptoms of depression and you say you are not depressed?"

I waited for the obvious to register, but it did not. She insisted she was not depressed. I left the meeting puzzled. How could a woman who looked depressed and who had most of the symptoms of depression not be depressed?

As unbelievable as this may sound, she is not atypical. I suspect that one of the reasons she didn't recognize her depression is our tendency to generalize and stereotype. If this woman had known that depression comes in varying degrees and intensities, she may have recognized it in herself. Familiarity with the types of depression will increase our power of observation and our ability to help ourselves and others.

So let's begin our look at the types of depression with what is called *normal depression.* We experience normal depression when we react with sadness and grief to life's stresses and losses. For example, when Sue returned to work after her August vacation, her coworkers noticed how pale she looked. She worked at her desk methodically without looking up. During breaks, she didn't smile or chat. No one could understand why this usually bubbly person was now sad. They urged Cathy, whom they called their "resident psychologist," to talk with Sue. Cathy found out that Sue's nephew had been killed in the collapse of some bleachers at the county fair. Sue had pulled him out of the rubble and had tried to resuscitate him.

When Cathy returned to the coworkers with this information, they understood the change in Sue. Her reaction was normal; any one of them would have responded the same way. When we lose our job, when a parent dies, when a close friend moves away, or when our children get in serious trouble — these circumstances result in feelings of helplessness and sadness. Usually our mood lifts in a few days or weeks. Some people who experience normal depression may feel the need for professional help. If they seek help, the diagnosis on the bill is adjustment disorder.

If symptoms of normal depression increase in number or severity or last an unusually long time, your mood may turn into what is called *clinical depression*—an umbrella term covering several different types of depression. Clinical depression sometimes results from external forces — traumatic experiences over which we have no control.

For example, Sandra had a terrible year when she turned forty. In the space of seven months, her father died, her husband moved out, and her sales decreased by 35 percent. Sandra started to have chest pains and tremendous headaches. She was convinced she was dying. In a way, she wanted to die. She felt she deserved what had happened to her. She didn't have the energy to cry, but she did have the energy to eat. She said, "I was trying to fill up the tremendous void at the center of my life."

After talking with several other medical doctors who couldn't find anything wrong with her, Sandra went to see a psychiatrist. He diagnosed her condition as clinical depression. Depression is labeled *clinical* when it needs treatment and when it is identifiable by certain established criteria.

MAJOR DEPRESSION

The most common type of clinical depression is *major depression*, sometimes called *unipolar depression* because it refers to one pole of emotional state, the lows. Major depressive episodes occur twice as often in women as in men.[1] The symptoms include the following:

+ Depressed mood most of the day, nearly every day.[2]
+ Markedly diminished interest or pleasure in all or almost all activities most of the day, nearly every day.
+ Significant weight loss or gain when not dieting or a decrease or increase in appetite nearly every day.
+ Inability to sleep or excessive sleeping nearly every day.
+ An abnormal speeding up or slowing down of activities and mental processes nearly every day, as observed by others. Merely feeling restless doesn't count.
+ Fatigue or loss of energy nearly every day.
+ Feelings of worthlessness or excessive or inappropriate guilt nearly every day.
+ Diminished ability to think or concentrate, or indecisiveness nearly every day.
+ Recurrent thoughts of death or suicide (with or without a plan).

Five of the symptoms must be present for a diagnosis of major depression. In addition, one of the five must be either a depressed mood or loss of interest or pleasure. The symptoms must be present during the same two-week period and they must represent a change from previous functioning.[3]

DEGREES OF SEVERITY

Major depression varies with individuals.

When a woman has a few of the symptoms—just enough to meet the criteria for major depression—and they cause minor impairment in social or occupational functioning, she has a *mild depression*.[4] For example, when Carol's normally patient husband blared on the car horn, she looked at her watch. They should have left for church twenty minutes ago. *What's wrong with me?* she thought. *I'm not usually this slow; I just couldn't decide what to wear. I don't have any energy, and I want to sleep all the time. God will probably strike me dead for thinking this, but I wish I didn't have to go to church. I don't get a thing out of it anymore.*

When you have nearly all the symptoms of major depression, and they markedly interfere with regular day-to-day activities, you have a *severe depression.* That was Dana's problem. She can't remember when her marital problems began. At first she seethed with anger. Now she felt numb and blank. She sat in front of the picture window, looking out at the activity on the street, yet she didn't really see what was occurring. She didn't eat and she didn't want to talk with anyone. She quit her job because she couldn't deal with people any longer. Even her children tiptoed around her as they fended for themselves. Dana was so miserable she wished she could die. *If I wasn't such a coward, I'd kill myself. I'm so incompetent that I can't even do that.*

The degree of severity in a major depression can go all the way to a complete loss of contact with reality (called a psychotic break). Most major depressions never reach the psychotic stage.

In between mild and severe depression is *moderate depression.* If you have a moderate depression you will have more symptoms than a person with mild depression, and the symptoms are often more intense. Your functioning will not be as impaired as with severe depression. You may cut back on some of your activities, but with extra effort you are able to keep up with the essentials.

WHAT'S THE DIFFERENCE?

The prevailing opinion holds that *major depression* is a disorder of the body and that *normal depression* is of no medical interest. Some experts disagree. Dr. Martin Seligman, a leading depression expert, is one of them. In *What You Can Change and What You Can't,* he writes, "I believe they are the same thing, differing only in the number of symptoms and their severity. One person may be diagnosed as having unipolar depression and be labeled a patient, while another with just the same symptoms may be held to be suffering from acute symptoms of normal depression and not be a patient."[5]

Either way, the body's neurochemistry is the same. Both major depression and normal depression involve changes in thought, mood, behavior, and the body. Both can make you feel miserable. Both can impair how you function in your day-to-day life and interact with others.

THE ROLLER COASTER ILLNESS

Bipolar depression, also known as manic-depressive disorder, encompasses two poles of emotional state, highs and lows.

People with bipolar depression have mood cycles—terrible "lows" (depression) and inappropriate "highs" (mania) that can last from several days to months. In between the highs and lows, they feel completely normal. The lows of the manic-depressive cycles are similar to unipolar depression. Mania is a psychological condition that looks like the opposite of the lows. It is characterized by some or all of the following symptoms:

+ Feeling unusually "high," euphoric, or irritable. (This symptom must be present for an illness to qualify as bipolar depression.[6])
+ Increased energy
+ Needing less sleep
+ Inappropriate excitement or irritability
+ Talking a lot or feeling the need to keep talking
+ Being easily distracted by unimportant or irrelevant details
+ Disconnected and racing thoughts
+ Impulsive behavior and poor judgment (spending too much money, inappropriate sexual activity, foolish business investments)
+ Inflated self-esteem or feelings of greatness
+ Making lots of plans for activities (at work, school, or socially) or feeling the need to keep moving

The first symptom plus three or four others must be present for a distinct period of time for a diagnosis of bipolar depression.[7]

During the manic phase of the bipolar cycle, a person denies that there are any barriers to realizing her dreams. She feels invincible, as though she can conquer the world. "The adrenaline rush of a manic phase leaves those who experience it feeling that life is terrific, people are wonderful, and no challenge is too great."[8]

Mania doesn't sound bad, does it? But the depressive crash after feeling on top of the world can be debilitating. Darkness and fatigue roll in. Intense high energy is replaced by a desire to do nothing. You feel defeated, especially when you consider the complicated consequences of impulsive behavior and poor judgment.

Bipolar depression is usually an inherited illness, although it can be caused by head injury or other medical conditions. Far less common than unipolar depression, bipolar disorder affects about one in 100 people[9] and is often a chronic recurring condition.

Bipolar depression affects men and women in roughly equal numbers.[10]

IF YOU DREAD THE FALL . . .

A thirty-one-year-old woman wrote, "I used to dread the fall. When the leaves dropped, my mood would, too. I'd see the first leaves on the ground and I'd panic. . . . I couldn't work; I wouldn't want to wake up; and I'd start putting on weight. I couldn't help it. Every fall I'd start this cycle that would last all winter. As soon as the days got longer and the green leaves started on the trees, I'd emerge again. . . . I often wished I was a bear so I could just go hibernate until spring. It seemed very sensible to me, and a lot less stressful than trying to maintain a regular life."[11] These words describe another type of clinical depression known as *seasonal affective disorder* (*SAD*). SAD is characterized by severe seasonal mood swings, typically hitting in late fall or early winter and lasting until the following spring when behavior returns to normal.

SAD afflicts about four times as many women as men[12] and usually appears in her twenties and thirties. Sufferers gain weight (they frequently crave carbohydrates), oversleep, become listless, experience fatigue, withdraw socially, lose interest in sex, and feel anxious and irritable. To qualify as SAD, you would have to seasonally experience these symptoms more than once. The symptoms must occur at least three different times, and twice in consecutive years.

The exact cause of SAD is uncertain. But many experts believe the reduced sunlight of winter may trigger a change in brain chemistry, since exposure to light (phototherapy) reverses SAD in most people. Just any kind of light won't do. Turning on more lamps in the living room or going to a tanning salon will not work. You need a special light box containing several fluorescent light tubes that emit the full spectrum of natural light at five to ten times (some sources say twenty times) the intensity of indoor lighting. SAD sufferers spend thirty minutes to five hours daily soaking up the light-box rays.

If you suspect you have seasonal affective disorder and want to try light therapy, you need to see a mental health professional. Once you have a diagnosis, the professional will assist you in getting a light box. Commercially available light boxes are advertised, but these "are not approved by the Food and Drug Administration; light therapy should be tried only under professional supervision."[13]

LIVING UNDER A SHADOW OF SADNESS

Dysthymia, which literally means "ill-humored," is a mild chronic depression. One psychologist compares it to a low-grade infection you can't get rid of; it stays and stays. Many people don't even notice when the symptoms begin. Often it's only when you've been treated and feel differently that you realize you've been living under a shadow of sadness and pessimism. Dysthymics tend to have interpersonal problems, poor self-esteem, and difficulty asserting themselves. Their symptoms can include any of the twenty listed in the last chapter, excluding delusions or hallucinations. The symptoms may be fewer than for major depression, and they are not as severe. The distinction is the duration of the symptoms. In dysthymia, the symptoms must have been going on for more than two years.

People with dysthymia tend to be chronically unhappy for much of their lives.[14] Losses and disappointments from your past are alive in the present, coloring your outlook. You feel more pessimistic than is necessary or appropriate. A Christian woman who is dysthymic finds it difficult to reach out and take hold of God's promises. She reasons, "It is far better not to hope than to be constantly disappointed."

With this pessimistic outlook, dysthymics are at risk for major depression. When people who have struggled with long-term dysthymia experience a major depression, the condition is called "double depression." "An estimated 3 to 4 percent of Americans—two out of three of them women—experience dysthymia during their lifetime."[15]

People with dysthymia "go through the motions" of daily life for years, often with little pleasure or enthusiasm. They may have lived under the cloud so long that it feels normal. Perhaps the woman I mentioned at the beginning of this chapter had dysthymia. This would explain why she looked depressed and had the symptoms of depression but insisted she wasn't depressed. She had nothing to compare it to.

Dysthymia is a recently identified type of clinical depression. If I had known about it at the time, I could have given this woman a label for what she was experiencing. She might have responded as one woman did when she was diagnosed with major depression. After worrying for weeks over what was causing her memory lapses and sleepless nights, she said, "It was a relief when the doctor told me I was suffering from major depression. Now I know there's a reason for why I feel the way I do." Understanding the different types of depression can direct women to appropriate resources. This book is designed to be a resource that focuses on major depression. From now on when I use the word *depression* I'm referring to major depression—whether mild (normal), moderate, or severe. Manic-depressives, SAD sufferers, and dysthymics can follow the guidelines for seeking professional help, but they may want to seek other resources for understanding why they feel the way they do.

Chapter Five

What Triggers Depression

W hile Robin's mother had been depressed several times, Robin never had until she discovered her husband of fifteen years was having an affair. She was unable to work efficiently or sleep soundly; she cried often and paced restlessly. It wasn't until a friend referred her to a psychiatrist that Robin realized she was depressed.

Robin's experience is typical. Although depression can occur without an apparent cause, most depressions are triggered by specific events or conditions.

STRESSFUL EVENTS

Topping the list of triggers is stressful events. A study of 680 pairs of female twins by researchers at the Medical College of Virginia, the Institute for Social Research at the University of Michigan, and Washington University School of Medicine (St. Louis, Missouri) ranked the importance of nine risk factors for major depression: genetic factors, parental warmth, childhood parental loss, lifetime traumas, neuroticism, social support, past depressive episodes, recent difficulties, and recent stressful life events. The women were assessed three times at greater than one-year intervals. The last two assessments included a structured interview evaluation for presence of episodes of major depression. While the researchers found evidence for genetic susceptibility, stressful life events posed a far greater danger. The study found that recent stressful events was the best predictor of depression.[1]

Stressful events can threaten our well-being, burden our ability to function from day to day, or require substantial readjustment of our point of view or daily activities.[2]

A divorce, a move, a job loss, a major failure, or a rejection might fit this definition, although what's considered a stressful event varies from person to person. A situation that requires substantial readjustment for one person might be a slight inconvenience for another. People who possess several risk factors (chapter 2) are less able to cope with stressful events. They can't roll with the punches as well as those who possess no risk factors.

Depression triggered by stressful events may not kick in immediately. When Betty's husband was fired from his job, she responded by being extremely supportive. She took on a second job until he found work again. After six months, (her husband was now employed), Betty's anxiety lessened and depression surfaced. She felt baffled. She could see no connection between her depression and his job loss, but her body could. She needed time to recover from the emotional fallout and from working two jobs.

LOSS

The most notable stressful event that triggers depression is loss, tangible or intangible.[3] Some examples of tangible losses are:

+ Death of a friend or relative
+ End of a marriage
+ Loss of income
+ Loss of position
+ Loss of material possessions (a home destroyed, valuables stolen).

Intangible losses aren't so obvious. They include loss of love, self-respect, values, beliefs about God, concepts about self, youth, and appearance. Intangible losses " . . . depend on our beliefs and values systems and can, of course, greatly differ in importance from person to person."[4]

Intangible losses can be as powerful a cause of depression as tangible losses.[5] In addition, intangible loss is hard to define, hard to talk about, and often hard to accept. Tangible losses engage the sympathy and support of friends and fellow church members; intangible losses often appear irrational or exaggerated to others.

Both tangible and intangible losses can be present at the same time. When Stephanie's first child died shortly after birth, she left the hospital with arms aching to hold the child she had carried inside for nine months. Her loss was very real, and her friends rallied to comfort her.

Long after the last casserole was delivered to the house, the intangible loss took hold. Stephanie mourned the loss of "what might have been," the hopes, the dreams, the plans she had for the child. She mourned the loss of the kind of mother she had planned to be. When she tried to talk about these things, her friends hushed her with, "You'll have another child." Maybe she would, but right now her intangible loss felt overwhelming.

CHRONIC STRESS

Stressful events—the kind that trigger depression—can usually be pinpointed to a specific moment: the night we broke up, the day my mother died, the day the factory closed. The specific time marker makes this trigger easy to spot. When stressful events occur, we can stay alert to our increased vulnerability to depression.

Another potential trigger of depression is harder to recognize because it doesn't have a specific time marker. These are chronic conditions we must endure over a period of time.

+ Friction with a rebellious teenage child
+ Caring for an emotionally disturbed or severely handicapped child
+ Caring for an invalid parent who shares your home
+ Persistent financial problems
+ Working for a boss who issues inconsistent instructions yet demands perfection
+ Living with constant pain
+ Persistent marital strain

The endlessness of these conditions takes its toll on our emotions and body. When Georgia's daughter moved back home with her three-year-old daughter, Georgia took a deep breath and thought, *I can handle this.* She was confident they would be able to make the adjustment. They did fine for the first year, but by then Georgia had expected her daughter to be out on her own again.

Georgia began to resent last-minute baby-sitting requests. Her job was demanding and she needed her evenings to unwind. She began to have difficulty getting up in the morning. Then she found herself not wanting to go to work; she wanted — no, she *craved*—time alone. Then a message started playing over and over on her internal recorder: *I don't know if I can go on any longer; I don't know if I want to try.* Although she couldn't pinpoint exactly when her depression arrived, it now held Georgia in its grip.

OVERLOAD

Not only does ongoing stress trigger depression, so does its weight. Life's responsibilities can get too heavy to carry.

Women who work and have a husband, children, or both, have multiple responsibilities. Most women who work outside the home still do most of the cooking, cleaning, and caring for children. They are also expected to be nurturing mothers, supportive wives, and efficient workers. These demands, and our striving to meet them, can lead to exhaustion and then depression.

If there's any one characteristic that defines the collective mood of American women at the end of the twentieth century, it's exhaustion. We are doing more than any generation before us as we adroitly balance the demands of work, family, and service to others. But we are paying a steep price. "More than half the burnout cases that make it into the doctor's office are depressed patients."[6]

UNREALISTIC EXPECTATIONS

We form expectations about our lives in childhood and adolescence. We plan and dream in accordance with those expectations. When we grow up, our expectations may or may not coincide with reality. When they do not, the harsh contrast between what we hoped for and what is, and the resulting disorientation we feel, can lead to depression.

For example, as a child Susie learned that sitting still and being obedient brought rewards. She listened well in class and memorized what her teachers said. Consequently, she made good grades. Without realizing it Susie developed the expectation that goodness is always rewarded.

This expectation was reinforced throughout high school and the small Christian college she attended. It even worked well on her first job when she simply followed orders. But when Susie moved into a management position, she lasted a year before getting fired because she didn't exercise initiative.

Susie cried for days; she felt as if a rug had been pulled out from under her. It had. The rug was her expectation that goodness is always rewarded. Susie's friends empathized with her about the job loss, but they were put off by her frequent crying. They thought she was overreacting. One told her, "You should have been smart enough to see it coming." That only made her more depressed.

An old dictionary definition of depression is, "sadness greater and more prolonged than warranted by any objective reason." Unrealistic expectations defy objective reason. That's what makes it difficult for us to talk about them and for people to understand why we are depressed. The more important an expectation is to us, the greater the pain of disappointment when it gets dashed.

PURSUIT OF THINNESS

Pursuit of thinness is mentioned as a separate trigger because it is noted by depression expert Dr. Martin Seligman[7] as one explanation for the difference in the depression rate between women and men. "Throughout the world, in every culture that has this ideal of thinness, depression is twice as common for women as for men, and there are more incidences of eating disorders."[8]

To a much greater extent than men, women in our society have been caught up in the notion that being very thin is beautiful. The thin ideal is biologically almost impossible to achieve, however. If you are one of the majority—dieting constantly to achieve the ideal—you are set up for depression. Either you will fail to keep the extra pounds from coming back, like 95 percent of women (and then failure and frequent reminders that you are "too fat" will depress you), or you will succeed and become a walking anorexic, starving constantly . . . and suffering one of the major side effects of starvation—depression.[9]

LACK OF MEANING

"At times depression may be due to feelings of meaninglessness and emptiness—an existential vacuum in life."[10] If a woman starts quoting Ecclesiastes, "All is vanity,"[11] she may have become acutely aware that her life lacks meaning. I know, because I've been there. From childhood I operated on the premise that God has a purpose for our lives. That premise made every detail of my life significant.

After several bizarre happenings that made no sense, I concluded that God didn't have a purpose for my life. A morning person by nature, I no longer wanted to greet the day or get out of bed. I had been a Christian for so long that I simply did not know how to live without a purpose. I floundered and became depressed.

Most people have a purpose, even though they may not be conscious of one. That purpose undergirds life, providing it with significance and meaning. If purpose gets lost, there can seem to be no reason to go on living. Those who experience this stress conclude, "Life is useless, all useless" (Ecclesiastes 1:2, TEV).

NO CONTROL

What's your outlook on life when you feel you have no control over what's happened to you in the past, what is happening now, or what will happen in the future? We feel helpless. While anyone can experience this feeling, there are some categories of women who typically experience this depression trigger.

Many *single mothers* are in this dilemma. Families headed by single women are among the poorest in the country. They must raise their children with little if any emotional and financial support, and they feel trapped.

Sexually or physically abused women may feel they have no control over their situations. Intimidated by their abusers, they lack self-confidence and often lack finances. So they stay in their abusive relationships.

Women who are sexually harassed on the job may not see a remedy to their situation. Quitting their jobs means facing the insecurity of looking for another one. Yet staying where they are usually means working in an intolerable and hard-to-change environment.

Women who frequently experience a sense of no control may expect situations in the future to be uncontrollable. They may not be helpless in their current situation, but they see themselves as helpless. This perspective leads to sadness, reduced motivation, and an inability to see opportunities for controlling future situations.[12]

Some depressions result from the belief that we have no control over important areas of our lives. This theory of depression is called *learned helplessness*. (More about this in chapter 8.)

UNEXPRESSED EMOTIONS

Grief, guilt, and anger often accompany the triggers listed above. If these emotions go unexpressed, they also can become a trigger for depression.

On the whole, grief, guilt, and anger are decent emotions; they all have their function. However, they are also unpleasant emotions to experience. Because they feel so terrible, we might be tempted to keep the lid on them rather than let them surface.

Grief, guilt, and anger also have a bad reputation. They are notorious for getting out of hand, and many books have been written on how to deal with them. If you pride yourself on being able to control these emotions, you might not express them when you need to. If you do express them, you fear they might get out of control, affecting how others see you or how you see yourself.

Some Christians assume that grief, guilt, and anger have no place in the life of a believer. This misbelief prevents them from expressing these emotions when they need to.

When we don't admit we have these feelings, and we deny or suppress them, we are ripe for depression.

Depression is like an emotional wet blanket that is used to put out uncomfortable emotional fires, many of which are negative feelings toward others. This equal-opportunity wet blanket, however, smothers positive feelings as well. The result is sadness, discouragement, boredom, loneliness, guilt, worthlessness, and hopelessness.[13]

WE ALL HAVE OUR LIMITS

Obviously, depression triggers are related to each other. Unexpressed grief and loss go hand-in-hand. Unrealistic expectations may add to the weight of chronic stress. Anger accompanies no-control situations. You may be completely resistant to a trigger on one occasion and quite vulnerable to it later. Its impact depends not only on its force but on your state of being at the time and whether you have enough support. Likewise, stress on top of stress makes us more vulnerable to depression than if we had sufficient recovery time between stresses. That may have been what happened to Naomi in the Old Testament story of Ruth. Naomi moved to a foreign country with her husband and two sons. The two sons married foreign women—Ruth was one. Then Naomi's husband and sons died. When Naomi returned to her home in Bethlehem, she didn't have any way to support herself. She asked her friends not to call her Naomi anymore (Naomi means pleasant). She said, "Call me Mara [bitter] because the Almighty has made my life very bitter" (Ruth 1:20).

Pain and disappointment happen to everyone, but some of us seem to buckle under more easily than others. Those of us with a lower tolerance for coping with painful life experiences appear to be predisposed to depression. The depression of women is a complex issue; it's hard to test for all the variables. Right now there seems to be no single, simple explanation for women's greater tendency than men toward depression, but there are many possible explanations. Those explanations have to do with our bodies, our relationships, our world, our thinking, and our past. If we are going to understand why we feel the way we do, then we will gain insight by exploring these five areas.

PART TWO

WHY DO MORE WOMEN THAN MEN GET DEPRESSED?

Chapter Six

What's Your Body Telling You?

～

When it comes to discussing differences between men and women, the first difference that comes to mind is a woman's unique function: the ability to give birth. The related hormones are often blamed for what women do and say. A woman is irritable with her husband. He chalks it up to PMS.

A woman is belligerent several times in a committee meeting. Afterwards, one member says to another, "She's probably going through menopause."

Women make similar assumptions about themselves. If you have a severe headache you might think, *Let's see . . . it must be time for my period.*

Do birth-related hormones provide an explanation for the difference in the depression rate between men and women? That's what we want to find out in this chapter.

DO I HAVE PMS?

As a flight attendant, Cheryl is expected to be bright, cheerful, and resourceful on the job—sometimes up to fourteen hours at a stretch. Cheryl can usually manage it. . . half the month. The other half, a mist descends, making her feel sad. Every smile and "Enjoy your flight" is forced, and she is exhausted when she returns to her apartment.

Some women experience depressive moods before menstruation. The development of physical and mood disturbances prior to menstruation is called premenstrual syndrome (PMS).

Besides depression, PMS symptoms include irritability, sore breasts, bloating, food cravings, exhaustion, headaches, crying spells, and dozens more. The number and variety of symptoms women experience differ from one woman to another and even with the same woman from one cycle to another.

Not all women experience premenstrual symptoms. Some women have mild symptoms, others have severe symptoms. According to the American Psychological Association National Task Force Report on Women and Depression, five percent of women experience significant discomfort and need professional help.[1]

Many experts say PMS results from hormonal changes in a woman's body. The suspect hormones are the estrogen and progesterone that rise and fall in different proportions between a woman's menstrual periods to regulate ovulation. Progesterone, known as the "quieting" hormone, appears to have some natural analgesic effects. Estrogen makes women feel happier, healthier, and optimistic. Before ovulation, the estrogen is dominant. It increases and peaks at ovulation. After ovulation, progesterone is dominant. The estrogen peaks again during this time, but progesterone remains dominant. Some four or five days before menstruation, progesterone takes a steep, abrupt nosedive. Estrogen, at the same time, falls rapidly, but not with the same steepness. The sudden diminishing of these hormones might be what makes women susceptible to depression and other disturbances right before menstruating.[2]

But the explanation may go beyond diminishing hormones. Estrogen and progesterone directly affect nerve cell functions, profoundly influencing behavior, mood, and the processing of sensory information—all of which are known to fluctuate during the normal menstrual cycle. One of the ways they do this is by modulating the action of neurotransmitters[3] such as serotonin and norepinephrine (see chapter 2), which are linked to depression. In the 1980s, several studies revealed that women who had PMS had lower serotonin levels right before their periods than women who do not have PMS.[4] Another possibility is melatonin. "Research at the University of California at San Diego found that some women who are depressed as a result of PMS have lower amounts of a brain chemical called melatonin when they sleep. Melatonin is released by the pineal gland to induce sleep and regulate circadian rhythms. Experts believe melatonin may suppress mood and mental quickness."[5]

Even if the exact explanation for it is not known, a woman can know if she has PMS by keeping a daily record of physical and emotional changes. She needs to develop this calendar for several months to see if it reveals a pattern of physical and mood changes almost every month before menstruation. If so, this is a time of vulnerability for her. She may experience any number of symptoms, one being depressive feelings. If a woman's symptoms are severe (suicidal thoughts, for example), she needs to seek medical help.

If the calendar reveals negative emotions that occur all month long but are intensified premenstrually, the problem might be a mood disorder such as depression.[6]

THE BABY BLUES

After the birth of Karen's first two babies, she was anxious to show them off. Full of energy, she took them both to church within a week of their births.

That's why she was surprised when she felt so shaky after the birth of her third child. Keeping up with the older two and the new baby overwhelmed her. Every time the baby cried, her whole body clenched. She worried about how this would affect the baby and didn't want to leave the house. The one day she did venture out with the baby in a stroller, she saw a dead squirrel in the street and immediately burst into tears. *Why am I crying over a dead squirrel?* she wondered. She concluded something must be terribly wrong, so she called her doctor. He explained that she was depressed. "Depressed! I can't be. I'm too positive of a person to be depressed." Her doctor explained that it happens to many new mothers. The birth of a child brings with it increased risks of emotional illness. A new mother is at risk for the "baby blues," postpartum depression, and postpartum psychosis.

Between 50 and 80 percent of all new mothers experience a brief transitory depression known as the "baby blues."[7] The onset occurs within the first ten days following the birth of the baby and often fades within a week. Symptoms include crying spells (often unpredictable and for seemingly trivial reasons), restlessness, irritability, anxiety, fatigue, headaches, self-dislike, confusion, guilt, and negative feelings toward the baby (and the father!).

The "baby blues" do not fade away for a sizable minority of post-partum women. Ten to 20 percent experience postpartum depression that lasts from six weeks to a year or longer.[8] Their symptoms are similar to any depressed person's symptoms (see chapter 3). What distinguishes postpartum depression from other depressions is a mother's anxiety over the baby's well-being and her inability to have normal maternal feelings. Postpartum depression can range from mild to serious. Mild depression includes bouts of feeling incapable, lonely, guilty, or frightened. These feelings appear and reappear, making it difficult to eat, sleep, and work. The feelings may be provoked by a specific incident, such as the baby crying all night or a talk with a childless, energetic friend.

When postpartum depression is severe, activities as basic as cooking, dressing, and caring for the baby seem impossible. Any woman suffering from serious postpartum depression should seek treatment for her sake and for the baby's.

A small number of new mothers (0.01 to 0.02 percent) experience a debilitating psychotic illness within six weeks of delivery.[9] In addition to feeling blue, a woman suffering from postpartum psychosis will experience extreme moods and agitation. She will hear and see things that others don't. She will be confused and perhaps have impulses to kill herself and/or her baby. She may feel she is being "ordered" to do things she normally would not do. Obviously, a woman with these symptoms urgently needs professional help and possibly hospitalization.

While symptoms for the "baby blues," postpartum depression, and postpartum psychosis are well documented, experts don't agree on the cause. Some say a woman's postpartum vulnerability has a biological basis; others say it is her life situation. Many biological changes do occur during pregnancy and after the birth of a baby. Estrogen and progesterone are present in generous and ever-increasing amounts in a woman's body throughout pregnancy. At birth, some of the estrogen is 100 times higher than it is during the last half of the menstrual cycle. Another estrogen is present at about one thousand times higher than during ordinary menstrual fluctuations.[10] During the last three months of pregnancy, a woman's progesterone level rises some tenfold from what it is during the second half of the menstrual cycle.[11] After delivery, estrogen drops dramatically and makes a slow return (anywhere from two weeks to twenty-one days) to nonpregnancy levels.[12] Progesterone drops to the point of almost being nonexistent.[13] This dramatic hormonal decline is similar to what happens four or five days before menstruation; only the drop is much greater at this time. Plummeting hormone levels that follow delivery may create a high-risk atmosphere for developing depression.

The new mother's moodiness and irritability, her tendencies toward depression and crying, may be similar to the symptoms one sees in a person coming off drugs (barbiturates, for example). In this case, of course, what would be occurring would be a female-hormone withdrawal.[14]

Added to hormonal changes are the changes in stress level. Fresh from delivery, a new mother is expected to work as hard or harder than she ever has and do it all on less sleep than normal.

The most vulnerable women are those experiencing multiple stresses, such as a job, financial problems, inadequate child-care, lack of close confidants, marital strains, illness of a family member, and illness or complications with the new baby. Her mate's behavior—more than any other single factor in her environment—seems capable of causing the mother's highly unstable mood to plummet.[15]

Perhaps the reason for a woman's postpartum vulnerability isn't one or the other—biology or stress. Perhaps it is a converging of the two. They arrive simultaneously and overload a new mother's circuits. Her energy shuts down. She needs time and help to recover.

DISMANTLING MYTHS ABOUT MENOPAUSE

Menopause signals the end of a woman's reproductive ability. It occurs, on the average, between the ages of forty-eight and fifty-five. Technically, menopause is accomplished when we have gone through an entire year without a menstrual period. But we sometimes attribute any number of things that happen to us in our forties to menopause. In one sense, we are right. Changes occur in our bodies long before our menstrual periods cease. During perimenopause, the eight years or so before a woman's periods end, ovulation becomes irregular and ceases. Consequently, the production of estrogen and progesterone slows down.

Depression in mid-life has often been blamed on declining hormones. But if that were the case, the rates of depression in women between the ages of forty-eight and fifty-five should be higher than those of younger women. They aren't. The rates of depression are highest among women twenty-five to forty-four.[16]

The decline in hormones associated with menopause is different from the hormonal vulnerability associated with PMS and postpartum vulnerability. In those cases, the hormones suddenly nosedive. The hormonal decline with menopause is gradual, so the body adjusts accordingly.

Though contemporary studies fail to prove that declining hormones cause depression, we hold that belief tenaciously. You may want to ask yourself the following questions before you accept that your depression is due to menopause.

1. *What stressful life events am I experiencing?* Depression in mid-life is often caused by multiple sources of stress, such as young adult children, ailing husbands, and aging parents.
2. *Am I bothered by aging?* As our periods become irregular, we are reminded that our options are closing. We notice our bodies are no longer as attractive as they once were, and our self-esteem suffers.
3. *How is my overall health?* In mid-life we become part of a group that begins to have health problems, something that increases with age. Chronic health problems trigger depression.
4. *What perimenopausal symptoms am I experiencing?* The increased irritability, poor concentration, and fatigue that many perimenopausal women report may simply be the result of sleep disturbances caused by hot flashes and night sweats. "In fact, when men were awakened and prohibited from entering deep sleep, researchers found them irritable and depressed."[17]
5. *Have I had my thyroid level tested?* One study of eighty-five perimenopausal women found that all those who were depressed had an underactive thyroid.[18] Hypothyroidism, as

the condition is called, mimics depression. We should be on the lookout for low thyroid levels because we are four times as likely as men to develop thyroid problems.[19]

While biological differences between men and women appear to contribute to the difference in their depression rate, they do not account for it completely. A premenstrual and postpartum vulnerability is evident, but these are ". . . probably not enough to make for a two-to-one ratio. Studies of premenstrual and postpartum emotion show that while hormones do affect depression, their effect isn't nearly big enough to create so large a disparity."[20]

Our unique function to give birth is clearly not enough to explain why women are more prone to depression than men are.[21] To blame the difference in the depression rate on hormones alone is simplistic and inadequate because it ignores other important facets of our lives, which we'll look at in more depth.

Chapter Seven

The People Connection

⟞⟞⟝⟝

While men and women are more alike than they are different, women tend to be more people-oriented. We see this as early as infancy. Female infants smile and start crying along with another baby more readily than do male infants. Baby girls babble more in response to the sight of a human face. One psychological study found that three-month-old female babies showed great interest in and paid attention to photographs of human faces. Three-month-old male babies couldn't quite discriminate between the photos and simple line drawings of faces. All stimuli seemed equally acceptable to the boys. The girls preferred photos of human faces.[1]

This responsiveness continues with girls. A study of 181 fifth-graders showed that the boys' games lasted longer than the girls'. One reason was that the boys' games required a higher level of skill and were less likely to become boring. Another reason was that the boys were able to resolve disputes more effectively than the girls. When disputes erupted, the boys enjoyed them as much as they did the game. "In contrast, the eruption of disputes among the girls tended to *end* the game."[2] The girls preferred to end the game rather than harm the relationships.[3]

In yet another study, young men and women in a class on moral and political choices were asked to describe themselves. All of the women were actively pursuing careers. Yet all of them described their identity in terms of relationships (wife, future mother, girlfriend). While measuring their strengths in terms of attachment ("giving to," "helping out," "being kind," "not hurting"), these highly successful and achieving women did not mention their academic and professional accomplishments.[4] In contrast, the men described themselves in terms of their achievements.[5]

Even the conversations of women reflect their orientation toward people. According to Dr. Deborah Tannen, author of *You Just Don't Understand*, the language of conversation for most women is a language of rapport. It is a way of establishing connections and negotiating relationships.[6] Tannen points out that for men, talk is for information, independence, and contest. For women, talk is for interacting with people and getting closer to them.

Being people-oriented contributes a rich and full life. Relationships add warmth, feeling, intimacy, color, and vitality to life. Women generally receive ". . . substantial satisfaction from their marriages, children, and friendships, and research finds that participation in such interpersonal roles and relationships is positively related to mental health."[7]

The flip side is that being people-oriented may also correlate to women's higher depression rate. I counted thirteen studies in *Women and Depression: A Lifespan Perspective* that connected women's greater vulnerability for depression to relationship issues.[8] Being people-oriented creates situations that are ripe for developing depression.

WHEN RELATIONSHIPS ARE LOST

Maggie Scarf writes in her comprehensive work on women and depression, *Unfinished Business: Pressure Points in the Lives of Women*, that when depressions happen in women, they happen in "one kind of context more than any other. This context is the loss of emotional relatedness. . . . *Attachments* are the critical variable: they seem to be, among both nonworking and working and highly professional women, what really *do matter most*."[9]

Both men and women resist any disruption of attachments. Neither of us give them up without anguish, but it is more powerfully true in the case of women.[10] Women invest so much in certain attachments that our very inner selves become intertwined with those to whom we are attached. Consequently, some of us do not—cannot—give up our attachments without great psychological or physical anguish.

Yet attachment losses and disruptions are a given in the lives of women. Many marriages end in divorce—most statistics say half. Children grow up to leave home. High mobility rates spell loss of extended family ties, friendships, and stable supports. Women generally outlive men by seven years, some statistics say eight years. You would think we'd get used to losses and disruptions, but we don't. We experience certain attachments so powerfully that we respond to loss or disruption with depression.

WHEN RELATIONSHIPS ARE STRAINED

"Although relationships can bring great satisfaction to women, problems and strains in such relationships constitute a greater risk factor for depression than problems or strains in other realms of life."[11]

Beth and Rachel were friends for years. Each married about the same time and had their children about the same time. They went through the stages of life together. "Nothing," they bragged, "could ever affect our relationship."

Maybe nothing ever would have if turmoil hadn't started at their church. The members polarized on what Beth considered a ridiculous issue. Rachel didn't see it that way. Every time Beth and Rachel got together, Rachel talked of the latest developments in the controversy. Sometimes she would call Beth at night, spewing out her anger.

Beth bristled. She didn't want any part of the controversy. She didn't feel comfortable listening to Rachel's harsh anger. Beth became depressed as she grieved over the loss of the way things used to be. Why couldn't she have her old friend back?

As difficult as a change in the quality and intimacy of a close friendship can be, strain in a marriage is a particular risk factor for triggering depression in women.

Marriage usually provides protection against depression. For both women and men, rates of major depression are highest among the separated and divorced, and lowest among the married, while remaining always higher for women than for men.[12]

The quality of a marriage, however, may contribute significantly to depression. Lack of an intimate, confiding relationship, as well as marital disputes, have been shown to be related to depression in women. In fact, rates of depression were shown to be highest among unhappily married women.[13]

Married women are three times more likely to be depressed than either men or single women.[14] "Within marriage, husbands more often than wives report being understood and affirmed by their spouses,"[15] yet women want to be understood and affirmed.

Men tend to hear women who discuss problems with them as requesting solutions, rather than simply looking for a sympathetic ear. When ironing out conflicts, many women feel, *The marriage is working as long as we can talk about it.* Husbands think, *The relationship is not working if we have to keep talking about it.* Discussing problems upsets some husbands; they prefer to arrive at a quick, practical solution. But wives want to 'talk the problem out' because that builds intimacy.[16]

ROLE OVERLOAD

"Women's role obligations to care for, support, and 'stroke' others can also heighten [their] risk for stress and depression."[17] When I shared that bit of information with a friend of mine in the nursing profession, she said, "Well, that explains the response at my workshop."

Judy presented a workshop on depression to an audience of male and female medical professionals. She passed out a questionnaire to determine if they were depressed. When she asked for a show of hands of those whose answers showed they were depressed, only women raised their hands. In particular, they were women with multiple roles—nurses, wives, and mothers—all of which required of them caring, supporting, and stroking.

Many of us become lifelong caretakers—first of our children, then of our aging parents, and possibly of our infirm spouses. For some of us, the stress and restrictions of being caretakers lasts most of our lives.[18] We tend to remain involved in the difficulties of our adult children and provide much of the care for elderly relatives. The average American woman will spend more years caring for parents than for her children.[19] The stress and restrictions of caretaking take a toll.

GREATER RANGE OF CARING

In relationships, women provide emotional support more frequently than men. We are life's informal counselors—the confidantes, the sources of affirmation, encouragement, and understanding for our children, teenagers, husbands, friends, aging parents, and sometimes our coworkers. As we "counsel," we often "catch" the stress of the people we help.

"Although men are distressed by events that happen to their children and spouses, women are distressed not only by these events but also by events which occur to other members of the social network."[20] Females are much more likely than males to perceive an event that involves someone else as a stress—either positive or negative.[21] We identify so intensely with others' stresses that we take them on as our own.

What we take on often includes what is not said. A woman is able to use both hemispheres of her brain to work on a problem. This ability makes her perceptive about people.[22] We sense the difference between what people say and what they mean, and we pick up the nuances that reveal another person's true feelings.[23] We can read the silences, sensing how another person feels.

Alma was really good at reading the silences. "When my husband first began pastoring," she told me, "I enjoyed sitting near the back of the auditorium during church business meetings. It gave me an entirely different perspective on what people really thought rather than just how they voted. Many times I could tell when people had hurt feelings—something my husband was often oblivious to. Now, after being deeply hurt in a couple of pastorates, I sit in the front. I no longer want to know what the people really feel. I can't handle their hurts and mine."

Because women are generally more sensitive to how people feel, and thus have a greater range of caring, they are at greater risk of depression. Their depression may be caused by:[24]

+ *Chronic stress*—Most people can handle taking care of others on a short-term basis, but many caretaking roles can go on for years. A woman may wonder, *Is this ever going to end?*
+ *Overload*—The weight of caring for so many may be too physically demanding. A woman can feel the weight when

she lies down to sleep at night. Her mind swirls with thoughts of all that must be done tomorrow, yet her energy is depleted.

✦ *Unexpressed emotion*—A woman may become angry over "having" to do so much for others yet be afraid to express it for fear of the consequences. Sometimes she feels guilty for being angry about caring for people. She thinks, *A person shouldn't resent caring for others. I'm selfish to be thinking of myself.*

✦ *Neglect of self*—Caring for so many increases the risk of depression, since caring for others may entail not caring for self.[25]

People have only so much physical and emotional energy in any given day, but women especially are expected to go the extra mile. "In family gender roles, such as wife and mother, and in community roles, such as neighbor and friend, women are expected to respond to the pain and the needs of others, whether or not their own needs for support and validation are met."[26] We may give out far too many love "currencies" from our emotional bank. When we continually give out more than we take in, the result is emotional bankruptcy that leads to depression.

ESTEEM EROSION

Many things about being people-oriented can eat away at a woman's self-esteem. Renowned West Coast counselor Dr. Archibald Hart says, "Anyone whose esteem has been eroded is likely to be more prone to depression."[27]

A woman's self-appraisal can become dependent on what others think. A college instructor I know gets depressed every June. Since Leah is a very effective, well-liked teacher, her students often give her a lot of positive affirmation. She thrives on their comments. Her family doesn't give her that kind of feedback. In fact, they give her very few positive comments. They eat the good meals she prepares without even look-ing up, let alone saying "thank you." Not one of them notices the neatly folded stacks of laundry she puts in their rooms or appreciates it when she gives up her time to listen to their problems.

When school is in session, Leah feels like a million. When it is not, she feels like a zero.

A woman's self-esteem can hang in the balance as she is torn about whom to please. Pleasing others can be complicated. One group wants one thing, and another something else. For example, many people in the adolescent's life expect her to follow the typical feminine route — dating, getting married, and planning for children. But she's also receiving messages about being independent and assertive, pushing toward a career. As one teenage girl said, "I'm expected to be competitive, pretty, smart, go to college, be an executive, and still be attractive to men."

Teenage girls aren't the only ones affected by this conflict. "Single women who are self-sufficient may nonetheless struggle with dependency conflicts and unmet emotional and relational needs."[28] Unmarried professional women may worry that a high-powered career will jeopardize their marital prospects.[29]

A woman may put the total blame of a relationship failure on herself. A woman's self-esteem is often heightened or diminished by the quality of her relationships.[30] When something goes wrong in a relationship, she reproaches herself. "If one has been disappointed, then the real causes lie in one's own unacceptability, inferiority, unworthiness, unlovability, and guilt (guilt, especially, about underlying anger at the other)."[31] With that kind of response, it's understandable why depression feeds on relationship failure.[32]

A woman's desire for attachments with people adds much to the richness of her life; I know it does to mine. At the same time, it makes us more vulnerable to depression. The way we respond to people, the way we need them, and the way we care for them has much to do with why we feel the way we do.

Chapter Eight

The Cultural Connection

~

The minute a baby is born, certain dynamics begin molding and shaping the gender of that new little person. If the doctor says, "It's a girl," certain expectations of how she should be and how she should behave are immediately activated. If the doctor says, "It's a boy," a different set of expectations are activated. Throughout childhood, those expectations will be replayed and reinforced time and again at school, at church, in the family, in social settings, through reading books and magazines, and through watching television. These expectations may vary from family to family, from ethnic group to ethnic group, from church to church, and from place to place, yet many are common to women.

Children also absorb cultural expectations by identifying with adults in their environment (usually someone of the same sex) and imitating their behavior. They learn how to be feminine and masculine.[1]

By the time a woman becomes an adult, these expectations take on the force of inner imperatives. They remind her of what is acceptable and unacceptable behavior. The imperatives are often accompanied by words such as *should, must, ought,* and *always.* Like neon lights, the imperatives blink on and off relentlessly, reminding women of what they ought to do.

"Because women in all contexts are more vulnerable to depression than men, it appears that certain cultural imperatives attached to being female are interacting with the developmental demands of adulthood to create symptoms of helplessness, low self-esteem, and hopelessness."[2]

In this chapter, we are going to explore how cultural expectations may contribute to a woman's depression.

PUT OTHERS FIRST

In the 1980s, Dana Jack, M.S.W., Ed.D., did a longitudinal study of twelve clinically depressed women. Rather than give the women questions with framed responses, she allowed them to speak in their own words. She writes, "I listened to their conflicts and concerns. . . . In the spirit of an anthropologist seeking knowledge of other cultures, I viewed these women as 'informants' from women's sphere."[3] She trusted they would locate and describe the stresses that rendered them vulnerable to depression.[4]

Jack's trust was rewarded. The women revealed they were trying to be good as defined by society: self-sacrificing and oriented to the needs of others.[5] They used words like *unselfish, giving,* and *submissive.* They put the needs of others before their own, especially their husbands' needs, whose wishes and interests came before theirs. But no one can be selfless all the time. When they "failed" they felt worthless as they evaluated themselves by societal standards.[6]

Guilt became their companion, hounding the women for not living up to the imperative to put others first. They tried harder. Their efforts, though, were not valued. Neither were they reciprocated; the women gave out far more than they received. They didn't gain the intimacy with their husbands they thought would result from their efforts to put them first.

These women experienced "a loss of self" in the process.[7] They had adapted to the needs around them so effectively that they experienced a loss of self within their roles of wife and mother.[8] Believing they couldn't be themselves, they constantly monitored their expressions,[9] keeping their thoughts, feelings, and needs to themselves.

Then they became angry. They were angry that their needs had not been met. They were angry at their husbands for not reciprocating. They were angry with themselves for abandoning their own feelings, thoughts, goals, and dreams.

They were angry at others—those unnamed people who through the years planted the imperative in their minds to always put others first. But what could they do with the anger? If they vented it, wouldn't someone get angry back at them? They "feared that if they tried to be themselves, they would lose their marriages; yet they described having lost themselves in an attempt to achieve an intimacy that was never attained."[10]

They came to believe they had to silence themselves if they wanted to stay in the relationship. If they expressed their feelings the relationship would end.[11]

Putting others first doesn't have to have the result that it did in the lives of these women. Putting others first is a biblical principle that laces living with graciousness and courtesy. It makes unselfish people out of selfish people. It improves relationships. It provides an avenue for ministry. I wouldn't want to live in a world that didn't emphasize putting others first. So how can a woman avoid losing herself as she puts others first?

One way is to view this imperative realistically. No one can be selfless all the time. Somehow or other, many Christian women feel as if they ought to be able to. They think, *If I were really good (or godly), I would always be able to put others first.*

Choosing to put others first goes a long way toward preventing depression. Choosing to put others first is a ministry. It's when we feel *obligated* to put others first that we become disgruntled. "Why do I have to be the one who always puts others first? Why must I always make the sacrifices? Why must I always be the first to apologize? When are they going to think of me?" As she counts the cost, a woman "begins to experience two opposing selves: an outwardly conforming, compliant self, and an inner secret self who is angry and resentful."[12] Jack suggests that it is at this point of inner division created by silencing the self in relationships that women are most vulnerable to depression.[13]

BE A TRADITIONAL MOTHER

Dr. Ellen McGrath presents a similar theory to Dana Jack's in her book on women and depression, *When Feeling Bad Is Good.* McGrath refers to the cultural imperatives as our traditional core. "The Traditional Core is a woman's cultural conscience, a core of traditional values and thinking that exists deep within every woman and dictates how we must behave and what roles are 'right' and 'wrong' for us to fulfill."[14] This core is stronger in some women than in others. Christian women will have biblical admonitions and teachings intermingled with the traditional values.

Part of the traditional core is our image of what a mother is. We believe a mother is someone who stays at home; a mother is warm and caring, always available. A mother smiles a lot, bakes cookies, fixes hot, healthy meals, always knows the right thing to say, and attends all of her children's athletic functions and school performances. This picture of a good mother is so entrenched in our culture that even a daughter reared by a woman who did not fit this picture may have it indelibly printed on her mind.

Carolyn, a school teacher whose mother was a school teacher, surprised me by saying, "I love my job. I believe I'm where God wants me to be. I wouldn't want it any other way; but I always feel guilty."

"About what? You're the last person I would expect to have a problem with guilt."

"Guilt over leaving my kids when they were small," Carolyn answered. "I stayed home with each of them a year, and then I just had to get back to teaching."

Even though she is an involved mother and her children are well adjusted, Carolyn still feels guilty. She has not lived up to her internalized picture for good mothering.

Carolyn, along with many others in our culture, has an internalized picture of the traditional stay-at-home, always-available mother. But our culture also expects women to be employed. Trying to be the perfect mother plus handling a demanding job can severely deplete energy. Rather than make choices and say no to part of the internalized mother image or become a less efficient worker, many women try to meet both expectations. They want it all. McGrath says that "having it all" puts women on a treadmill. "We run in place until we drop into depression."[15]

You would think women who work full time at fulfilling this image would be highly praised, but they aren't. Full-time mothers report being made to feel like they have to apologize for their choice or they have to defend it — a situation ripe for developing low self-esteem.

BE ATTRACTIVE

Part of our humanity — built in by God — is the desire to be attractive. It's the chemistry that draws men and women together to marry and have their social needs met. Most of us want to be attractive and we put some effort into it. The problem comes when we try to live up to impossible standards.

Dr. Ellen McGrath writes, "The pressure to be physically perfect and remain forever young are two of the most consistent sources of depression among women."[16] Both of these concepts are unrealistic and unattainable.

As a consequence of this propaganda, many tend to equate a woman's value with physical attractiveness. If a woman can't slither into a size 10 dress, she is undisciplined, unattractive, and unworthy. Even when a woman resists or rejects this message, it can still haunt her.

Women are expected to look young while their bodies are continually aging. They can do many things to be physically fit and to live longer. They can do things to slow down the aging process, but aging is a fact of life.

Chronic dieting has become a lifestyle for many women. Dieters fail much more often than they succeed. Women diet twice as much as men,[17] and interestingly, they have twice the depression rate of men.

When we can't reach the standards of looking youthful or being thin, we feel like failures. We *ought* to be able to do better. "It's just a few short steps from constantly feeling like a failure to becoming a depressed patient."[18]

ONE WAY OR THE OTHER

To each of these three imperatives, women often respond with absolutist, either/or thinking. You may have noticed this tendency yourself. Here are some of those messages:

+ Either care for your husband or care for yourself.
+ Either be thin and young or be unattractive.
+ Either be a traditional mother or be a poor mother.

Where in their thinking was there room for compromise? Isn't it possible for a woman to have an intimate relationship with her husband and be an authentic person? Isn't it possible to be overweight and attractive? Isn't it possible to be an attractive elderly woman? Isn't it possible to be a nontraditional mother and still raise well-adjusted children?

The answer to all of these questions is "yes," but many women in these situations see themselves as helpless. The imperatives are so strong, women may not have the energy to fight. Imperatives on how one "should" think and feel throws a wet blanket over the inner world of feeling and dampens its vitality.[19]

Even though these cultural expectations to be unselfish, giving, nurturing, and attractive are unrealistic, many women fear backlash if they take action: "If I assert my rights, I'll be called selfish." They fear losing relationships: "I might hurt his feelings, and I don't want him angry with me." "If I gain weight, my husband might leave me." They resist the hassles of negotiating change: "I can't stand conflict. I want a peaceful atmosphere in my home."

This helpless response may also have a cultural connection. In many cultures, females are socialized to respond with helplessness, passivity, and by giving up and accepting it, but men are taught to fight, challenge, and endure.

> Boys' behavior is lauded or criticized by their parents and their teachers, while girls' is often ignored. Boys are trained for self-reliance and activity, girls for passivity and dependence. When they grow up, women find themselves in a culture that deprecates the role of wife and mother. If a woman turns to the world of work, she finds her achievements given less credit than men's. When she speaks in a meeting, she gets more bored nods than a man would. If despite all this she manages to excel and is promoted to a position of power, she is seen as being out of place.[20]

Consequently, many girls and women come to expect little control over the events in their lives. They believe that whatever they do doesn't matter. "Learned helplessness manifests itself at every turn, and learned helplessness reliably produces depression."[21]

Perhaps the issues of low self-esteem and learned helplessness could be prevented if women were given more positive support in our culture. What a woman does is often undervalued because it's "women's work." Her contributions and comments as a woman may be overlooked because she is female. Despite recent changes in many areas, this under-valuation is still going on.

As the message of worthlessness gets repeated in subtle and sometimes not so subtle ways, it imprints itself on the mind of the young girl: *What you do doesn't count.* Without even realizing what happened, she picks up and internalizes the message.

Those three words, "It's a girl" and "It's a boy," wield so much power. Women who suffer from depression might benefit from taking time to consider whether these expectations play a part in their depression.

Chapter Nine

Responses to Trouble

Once after a major move, our family had $100 left and six weeks to go until payday. God provided for us in wonderful, surprising ways. Thrilled by God's response, I wrote an article describing our situation and His provision. The article was rejected again and again. I couldn't understand why, so I asked a friend to critique the article.

After reading it, Pat said, "You've overstated your situation. It was not catastrophic."

Pat's comment was an eye-opener. She was right. Our lives were never in real danger, but why had I felt they were?

I realized I had started to brood over our situation when our money began dwindling weeks before the move. The more I brooded the more anxious I felt, and the more fervently I prayed. I worried so much that our situation took on catastrophic proportions. No wonder I was thrilled when God delivered us!

Later I realized how my tendency to brood exacerbated my struggles with depression.

TWO RESPONSE STYLES

Most people have a habitual style of attempting to regulate their moods following a stressful event. Two predominant response styles are ruminating and distracting.

Ruminating means "chewing the cud." Animals, such as cattle, sheep, and goats, chew a cud composed of regurgitated, partially digested food. They chew it over and over. Ruminators hold up the event and view it from every angle. They make interpretations about the event. They examine their feelings about it. They focus on the possible causes and consequences. Their thoughts seldom include any action statements. In contrast, distracters respond to life's setbacks by distracting themselves through activities or others means. People with this style tend to act rather than reflect.

Of the two responses, ruminators are more prone to depression. Their ruminating style stokes their melancholy by amplifying and escalating it. A distracting response dissolves depression. The tendency to act breaks it up.[1]

GENDER DIFFERENCES

Sex differences in depression may be attributable, at least in part, to sex differences in response styles. When trouble strikes, men tend to act, women tend to think.

> When women rate what they actually do (not what they should do) when they are depressed, the majority say, "I tried to analyze my mood" or "I tried to find out why I felt the way I did." The majority of men, on the other hand, say they did something they enjoyed, like sports or playing a musical instrument, or they say, "I decided not to concern myself with my mood."[2]

While a distracting response can lead to other problems because it may be a form of denial, it will not directly cause depression. Moreover, a ruminating response style doesn't always spell depression. It usually depends on whether the ruminator is a habitual optimist or pessimist.

Optimists who are confronted with a bad event tend to believe it's just a temporary setback, that its causes are confined to this one event and the setback is not their fault.

Pessimists tend to believe that bad events will last a long time, will undermine everything they do, and are their fault. Pessimists give up easily. People with pessimistic patterns of thinking can transform mere setbacks into disasters.

PATTERNS OF THINKING

Cognitive distortions can produce depression and anxiety. I became familiar with them through Dr. David Burns's classic book, *Feeling Good: The New Mood Therapy*. Since then I have read variations of the patterns by other authors. Let's look at some of them.

1. *All-or-nothing thinking:* Personal qualities are evaluated in extreme black-or-white categories. When a straight-A student received a B-plus on an exam in my class, she was visibly upset. When I tried to tell her there was nothing wrong with a B-plus, she said, "You've either got it or you don't."

A B-plus said to Marsha that she didn't have it. Making an A meant success; anything less meant failure.

All-or-nothing thinking causes a woman to fear any mistake or imperfection because she will see herself as a loser. Then she will feel inadequate and worthless.

All-or-nothing thinking is unrealistic thinking. No one is absolutely perfect or totally incompetent. No one is completely attractive or totally ugly.

If we try to force our experiences into absolute categories, we will be constantly depressed because our perceptions will not conform to reality. We'll never measure up.

2. *Overgeneralization: Never, always, every,* and *all* are favorite words of ruminators who overgeneralize.

Jill was passed over for the promotion she had been praying for. She concluded, "I'll never get ahead in this business." Susan was late three times, and her friend, Kate, concluded that "Susan is always late. She is so disrespectful of my time." Twice Carol dropped bites of her salad while attending important dinners — once at a church banquet and once at a company dinner. Carol stopped eating salad at important occasions. "Every time I eat salad in public I drop some of it on me. I'm so clumsy."

Georgia was rejected by a young man she had been dating for six months. He said he didn't want to be committed to one person in a dating relationship. He wanted to be free for a while. As Georgia wished him well, she was thinking, *All men are jerks. I'm never going to find anybody to marry.*

3. Mental filter: A negative detail is selected and focused on almost exclusively until the whole is perceived as negative. The positive gets filtered out.

A family of three took a vacation together. The second day out, the husband and wife had a disagreement about where to stop for lunch. The disagreement escalated into an all-out argument. The rest of the trip went smoothly, but several days after they returned home, they had another squabble. They concluded, "We quarrel all the time. We couldn't even take a vacation without fighting for the entire trip." To their surprise, their twelve-year-old daughter who had gone with them pointed out they had quarreled only once during the seven-day trip. They had blotted out the good part.

4. Poisoning the positive: This thinking pattern takes a positive experience and transforms it into a negative one.

Marion stopped by to see her mother on her way to work. She was wearing a new dress. Her mother noticed and said, "How nice you look!" Marion thanked her, but mentally she discounted it. "She's just saying that because she's my mother. The girls at the office won't like it." With one swift blow she mentally disqualified her mother's genuine compliment.

Dr. David Burns writes that if a person constantly throws cold water on the good things that happen, no wonder life seems damp and chilly.[3]

5. Jumping to conclusions: When Judy and I were team teachers for a class of single young adults, ages eighteen to twenty-five, the class had a visitor one Sunday morning when I wasn't there. The visitor possessed a good grasp of the Bible and was outspoken. She and Judy clashed over a minor point. When the visitor never returned, Judy said, "I shouldn't have disagreed with her. I know that's why she didn't come back. I came on too strong."

"Why don't you give her a call and see?" I said.

Judy did, and the young woman was not bothered by the difference of opinion at all. She said, "I never returned because I felt too old for the class. I'm twenty-nine."

Elijah also jumped to conclusions when he was depressed after his cosmic duel with the prophets of Baal on Mount Carmel. When Elijah reminded God how unfaithful his fellow Israelites had been, he said, "I am the only one left," implying that he was the only one faithful to God

(1 Kings 19:10,14). God reminded Elijah that seven thousand Israelites had been faithful and had not bowed down to Baal (verse 18). Elijah was hardly the only one.

6. *The binocular trick:* In this cognitive distortion, a person looks at herself and others through a pair of binoculars. One end magnifies (blows up) the view, and the other end minimizes (reduces) the view. When she looks through the end that magnifies, she sees her own errors, fears, or imperfections and exaggerates their importance. "I made a mistake. How terrible! How awful! What will my friends think!" Through the magnifying end of the binoculars, a woman's faults appear gigantic and grotesque.

When a woman looks through the other end of the binoculars she sees her strengths. They always look small and unimportant to her. She minimizes her good qualities.

7. *Catastrophizing:* "Some people can put their troubles neatly into a box and go about their lives even when one important aspect of it — their job, for example, or their love life — is suffering. Others bleed all over everything. They catastrophize. When one thread of their lives snaps, the whole fabric unravels."[4]

This was what I did when our move left us short of money. Those who catastrophize respond to difficult situations by giving them nightmarish dimensions.

8. *Emotional reasoning:* In this cognitive distortion, negative feelings guide our actions. We take our emotions as evidence for the truth: "I feel it, therefore it must be true."

Examples of emotional reasoning include: "I feel guilty; therefore, I must have done something bad." "I feel helpless; therefore, my problems must be impossible to solve." "I feel exhausted; therefore, I can't go to work today." Feelings, however, are not always reliable.

After Casey got her children off to school, she went back to bed. "I feel so lousy. I just can't think about this messy house. Cleaning it today would be impossible." Thirty minutes later, the phone rang. It was a close friend who worked in sales in another city. "I'm going to be passing through your city later today," Kay said. "Would it be all right if I stopped by for an hour or so?" Ashamed to admit to her confident friend how lousy she felt, Casey said, "Yes, of course." As soon as she hung up, Casey thought, "I'll pick up in the living room, stash the breakfast dishes in the dishwasher, and spruce up the bathroom. If I close the hall doors to the bedrooms, maybe that will be enough to make the house presentable." Doing those things turned out to be quite gratifying and not as tough as Casey thought. Spurred on, she ran the vacuum cleaner and swept the kitchen floor. She then showered and put on her favorite slacks. When Kay arrived, her first question was, "How are you?"

"I'm feeling pretty good today," Casey said.

9. *Personalization:* We assume responsibility for a negative event when there is no basis for doing so. If a child's report card is bad, the mother who personalizes concludes, *I'm a bad mother.* If a patient doesn't follow instructions, the nurse who personalizes thinks, *I must be doing a lousy job. It's my fault the patient isn't working harder to help himself. It's my responsibility to make sure he gets well.* Dr. David Burns says that personalization causes a woman to feel crippling guilt. She suffers from a paralyzing and burdensome sense of responsibility that forces her to carry the whole world on her shoulders.[5]

These nine patterns of thought illustrate distorted ways of thinking that can become habitual and contribute to depression. Women may not be aware these thoughts are influencing their feelings. "Most people believe their emotions stem directly from what's going on around them. They pay no attention to the fleeting thoughts that connect situations to emotions."[6]

Cognitive distortions are quick, automatic thoughts that are so well practiced as to be almost unnoticed. You can identify your response style by observing how you respond the next time a stressful event occurs in your life. If you ruminate, see if your ruminations are optimistic or pessimistic. Your answer will show you if you're vulnerable to depression.

Chapter Ten

When the Roots Grow Deep

⤞

Painful experiences early in a girl's life—when she has no control over them—may grow tough roots deep into her adult life. Other tough roots grow when women have some control but don't recognize it or exercise it. Either way—control or no control—women need to know about tough roots to understand why they feel the way they do.

RELATIONSHIP WITH PARENTS

A girl's sense of being an all-right person of value comes, initially, from the loving relations she experiences within her family. Some children are blessed with a childhood that provides them the stamina and ego strength to engage life. Other children aren't so fortunate. They aren't loved and cared for. They are made to feel inadequate and told they will never amount to anything. They are shamed for the way they look or demeaned for stating their opinions. Most children reared like this will grow into adulthood with a lack of positive self-esteem.

The mother who exudes love unconditionally, who gives her child the full-bodied and reliable mother-warmth that child craves, despite all the turmoil and irritation of the day, has provided her with a basis of self-feeling she will carry throughout life. If mother-love is thwarted by circumstances or lack of enthusiasm, a child can be emotionally maimed for life.[1]

A father gives his daughter confirmation of her desirability as a female and affirmation of her value as a person. The way he treats her communicates to her his pleasure in her femininity.[2] As a girl's consciousness of self develops, she needs her father's continual affirmation that she is a worthwhile person. If she is denied his companionship and the esteem he can give her, she may question her worth.

LOSS OF A PARENT

If a mother's love and a father's affirmation are sorely needed for good mental health, then obviously the absence of one parent could have a devastating effect. Women who lose a parent when they are children, especially their mothers, are more likely to develop serious psychiatric problems, to become psychotically depressed and suicidal.[3]

The death of a parent is hard for a child to understand. Grief goes unexpressed because a child doesn't know how to acknowledge the loss. Many children feel angry and repress it. The child may be angry at the parent for leaving or angry with God for taking her parent away. Early loss makes a person more vulnerable to later losses in life.

Divorce, too, has its consequences. Some depression will be present in a child of divorce, even when the divorce is desirable and necessary.[4] A child may become depressed over the confusion and uncertainty she feels. She may think, *I must have been bad to make Daddy [or Mommy] go away.* If one parent drops out of the child's life after the divorce, the long-lasting effect can be the same as if that parent died.

A LEARNED PATTERN OF DEPRESSION

A child of divorced parents may become depressed because she identifies with a parent's depression.

Vijayakumari was in the study lounge looking at a recent group picture of the dorm residents when Barb joined her to study chemistry. Barb's grades were slipping and she needed someone more motivated to study with. She was so listless lately. She blamed it on the mysterious pain in her right side. She had gone to the doctor at the University Health Services, but he could find nothing wrong. Worry over what could be wrong affected her sleep. She was waking up every morning around 4:00.

As Vijayakumari looked up from the dorm picture she told Barb, "Your eyes are so sad."

"What? Let me see." Sure enough, her eyes were sad in contrast to the smiling eyes of the other girls.

Barb was startled by the way the picture had captured her expression and by Vijayakumari's words. When she was a little girl, Barb had said those same words to her mother in the months following her divorce. Barb's mother would then smile slightly, pat her on the shoulder, and say, "I'm fine, dear. Really I am." Although Barb was only eight, she also noticed how little her mother ate and how often she found her mother staring off into space.

At Barb's next doctor's appointment, she said, "I don't know if this means anything, but someone told me I have sad eyes."

"Well, are you sad?" he asked.

Involuntarily tears trickled down her cheeks. "Well, I guess I have been a little bit sad. The stress of the semester is incredible. My chemistry class is so difficult. I'm really disappointed in myself. I thought I would do better in college, and now I'm finding it hard just to keep at it. I had such big plans."

"I'm going to prescribe an antidepressant for you," the doctor said, "and I recommend that you start seeing a counselor at the university's counseling center. After six weeks, if you still have the pain in your side, we'll do some tests." In three weeks, Barb's mood had improved, and by four weeks the pain in her side was gone. One plausible explanation for Barb's experience is that she learned to be depressed from her mother. Children learn from their families how to handle stressful situations. "Individuals who spend their entire childhood identifying with negativistic, chronically depressed parents are going to learn similar attitudes."[5]

We learn by observation and example, and most of us model our behavior, attitudes, and thought patterns after our closest relatives. We intuitively experience their unspoken sad feelings and sometimes even unconsciously absorb their depressions as a way to be closer to them.[6]

If one of your family members felt helpless to solve life's problems, then you may have developed a helpless approach too. If he or she saw the world as cruel and unsupportive, you may see it as cruel and unsupportive. If one of them tended to be pessimistic and brooding, you may face life the same way.

The theory that an adult's depression may be a learned response is challenged by some experts. They point out that parents who suffer from depressive tendencies are more likely to be withdrawn, critical, inconsistent, and irritable in child-rearing. As a result, some children react to this difficult atmosphere by developing intense, exaggerated feelings of guilt—an avenue for developing depression.[7]

Other challengers say that the repeated depressive patterns in family members is passed along in the genes. Identical twins reared apart are far more similar as adults than fraternal twins reared together for qualities related to depression.[8]

Whatever the explanation—learned response, guilt reaction, or genes—being the child of a depressed parent may double or even triple the risk of depression in later life.[9]

A learned depressive response to life feels normal to the woman who has it. As far as she knows, everyone responds to life that way. As she struggles to understand why she feels the way she does, it doesn't occur to her there could be another, healthier response to life. It's a tough root to eradicate, and so is the root of physical or sexual abuse.

THE ABUSE LINK

Dr. Eileen Hoffman writes that whenever a woman in her office seems depressed or anxious or has multiple unspecified complaints, she starts asking questions about the patient's personal life. "Depressive symptoms," she writes, "can sometimes be a clue that some form of physical, sexual, or verbal abuse is occurring in a woman's life, or has occurred in the past."[10] Fifty percent of all psychiatric patients have childhood histories of severe chronic physical and/or sexual abuse.[11] Thirty-seven percent of women have a significant experience of physical or sexual abuse before the age of twenty-one.[12]

Women who have been abused often suffer from mood disorders that persist for a long time. Some of the abuse may cause neurological changes that result in depressive symptoms, but in most cases the depression is attributed to victimization. These women are defeated by helplessness, rage, and self-blame.

Sexual abuse may be a key explanation for the differences in the depression rates of men and women. "Before adolescence, boys are somewhat more likely than girls to be depressed, but by age 14 or 15, girls are much more likely than boys to be depressed."[13] Adolescence is a time of increased sexual abuse. In a random sample of 930 adult women, 12 percent had experienced some type of serious sexual abuse by a family member before age seventeen and 26 percent had experienced serious abuse from someone outside the family by that time. Several researchers have found that girls from age fourteen to fifteen have the highest risk of being raped of all age groups.[14]

American Health magazine reported that "a 1991 Stanford University study attributed up to 35 percent of the discrepancy between male and female depression rates to sexual abuse of women in childhood."[15] Another study found that over half the women who sought therapy for depression as adults in one clinic had been sexually abused as children.[16]

Many women never talk about the abuse they've experienced so their wounds have little chance to heal. Dr. Hoffman described an encounter with Kathy, a patient she was treating for high blood pressure. Kathy showed up at Hoffman's office one day, several weeks before her scheduled physical, saying she wanted to check on her blood pressure. Hoffman says her antennae went up right away and she suspected there was more to it.

As Hoffman probed, Kathy began talking about a friend who had been abused sexually as a child. As she spoke, tears rolled down her cheeks and she had a hard time maintaining her composure. Hoffman took a chance and asked, "And did that happen to you?"

Then Kathy told Hoffman what was really troubling her. "When she was a child," writes Hoffman, "her father had sexually abused her. Recently her own daughter had given birth to a child and she was terrified about her son-in-law being left alone with the baby. All of the feelings that had been locked inside for so long were flooding back."[17]

Kathy told Hoffman she had never spoken about this to anyone. For most of her adult life she had blocked it out. But with the birth of her grandchild, she couldn't cope with her feelings any longer. Her early childhood wounds had not healed.

Circumstances such as uncaring parents, lack of a mother's love, lack of a father's affirmation, loss of a parent, learned response, and abuse are all out of a woman's control. Some tough roots, however, take hold even when women have control. They develop from uncompleted growing tasks, unexpressed emotions, unsolved problems, and unresolved spiritual issues.

UNCOMPLETED GROWING TASKS

Each stage of life has tasks to complete before moving on to the next stage. If these tasks aren't completed a woman may be depressed about something she should have dealt with at an earlier stage.[18] For example, some young women never really achieve a healthy separation from home base. A healthy separation means that a woman lives in terms of meeting her own goals and setting her own standards. An unhealthy separation means she is still trying to please her parents. This was true for Stacy.

Maybe Stacy would have made the separation from her home base if she hadn't lived a block away from her parents in Rantoul, Illinois, after she married Sam. She and her mother had coffee every weekday morning. They talked on the phone frequently. Her mother helped her pick out the children's clothes. She and Sam never made a major purchase without getting her father's opinion. Then Sam was transferred to Seattle, Washington, to a position where he would have to do a lot of traveling. When Sam told her, Stacy had to sit down. She felt like the air had been knocked out of her.

Sam knew that most people get upset about moving, but they eventually reconcile themselves to it. Stacy didn't. When he wanted her to fly to Seattle to look at houses, she said the baby had a cold and needed her nearby. When he wanted her to help pack, Stacy said they needed larger boxes. When he came home from work, he often found Stacy in bed with the shades drawn. He had never seen her like this, and he was genuinely puzzled by her behavior.

What he didn't know—what Stacy hadn't even realized yet—was that she felt terrified of leaving her parents. The separation that occurs in a young person's life and results in an independent, autonomous sense of self had never occurred in Stacy's life. She defined who she was in terms of her parents, and she felt helpless to survive on her own resources away from them.

UNEXPRESSED EMOTIONS

While uncompleted growing tasks may cause depression, so can unexpressed emotions. It's like having an unpaid bill. If you've ever had a bill you were reluctant to pay, then you can relate to this tough root.

Perhaps you bought something on credit and then your financial situation changed. You needed the money for something else so you put off paying the bill. The notices, one after another, start to stack up. Eventually a bill collector calls, demanding payment.

Sometimes depression is a bill collector that says, "You have an emotional bill to pay."

An article in *McCall's* magazine told about an army nurse who didn't deal with the grief she experienced while serving in Vietnam. Later, back in the United States, married and with two children, she didn't understand why she felt sad. The way she described it, she had everything— two great kids, a beautiful home, a nice dog and three cats. She writes, "Anyone looking at my life would have said, 'That gal has it all! She must be happy as a clam.' But sometimes, when we were all snuggled up together watching TV, I'd wonder why I felt sad instead of joyful. Was I just a depressed person?"[19]

Because she was depressed and didn't know why, she made the mistake of thinking her family needed to shape up. She overreacted to normal childlike behavior. As she became increasingly edgy and afraid, she sought professional help and discovered that her depression was due to unexpressed emotions over events that happened years earlier in Vietnam.

UNSOLVED PROBLEMS

A tendency similar to not expressing emotions is putting off solving problems. The problem may be particularly tedious, too complicated for a quick or easy solution. It may involve confrontation, something many women are uncomfortable with. But putting off solving a problem is like stuffing things in the hall closet.

When you clean house, the smart thing to do when you pick up clutter is put it where it belongs or discard it. But the easy approach is to toss it in the hall closet. The living room looks better and the items are out of sight. One day, though, when you open the closet, everything tumbles out.

Our inner self is like a closet. We may handle some problems, such as difficulty with a child, a spouse, or coworker by shoving the problems in our inner closet. The relationship looks clean on the outside, but inside a mess is piling up. The day depression arrives is when everything tumbles out. The depression is signaling the need for some problem-solving.

UNRESOLVED SPIRITUAL ISSUES

Going against our value systems, what we know to be right and wrong, can eventually develop into a tough root of depression. Sin is deceptive, and it can deceive us into thinking there was just cause for what we did. The circumstances made it seem right.

Holding grudges, nursing resentment, and refusing to forgive are spiritual issues particularly conducive to depression. They are silent sins—known only to ourselves. It's hard to admit them. They often involve the actions of another person—the one we begrudge or resent or can't forgive. To let the resentment go or to forgive feels like we're letting the other person off the hook when he or she should be punished.

These silent sins lend themselves to ruminating; the Bible refers to it as cherishing or regarding iniquity (Psalm 66:18). By their very nature silent sins fan out, filling our inner spaces, securing a firm hold. When the sleepless nights come or our stomachs have pains for which the doctor can't find a reason, family and friends may sympathize and wonder why we suffer needlessly. We can't seem to make a connection between our depression and our unresolved spiritual issues. Depression is not a sin, but depression may be the result of sin.

The reason why a woman feels the way she does may go back a long way. Depression's tough roots—whether from outside influences or from within—are long and deep. But though it's difficult to eradicate them, it is not impossible. Help is available.

PART THREE

WHAT CAN I DO TO BEAT THIS ILLNESS?

Chapter Eleven

Do You Want to Get Well?

⤳

Fighting depression is war. The best ammunition we have is the knowledge that we will probably win the fight. Depression often retreats on its own if given enough time. The miserable feelings, the hopelessness, and the agony will leave. But if the depression doesn't lift on its own, there are many treatment options.

The knowledge that you will win over depression should be reassuring, but don't be naive about the enemy. Depression is powerful. Left unchallenged, it can cause a lot of damage.

WHY FIGHT IT?

Depression makes a woman miserable. Depressive episodes last between three and twelve months. If you really don't want to be miserable that long, you have to fight.

Depression impairs judgment. A depressed person's thinking patterns are distorted. Consequently, you may make disastrous mistakes while depressed—even quit your job or walk out of your marriage. When the depression lifts, you look back and think, *How could I have done such a thing?* Not to fight depression is to take a chance on doing something you'll regret later.

Depression sets a woman up for unnecessary hurt. Feeling bad turns into a magnet that attracts more hurt. Candace had one of those hard-to-talk-about depressions. She was grieving over reaching forty and still not being a success at anything. When she tried to talk about it to a friend, the friend said, "Oh, you are too successful." Candace didn't mention it to anyone again. When the school called about sending her son to detention for a week, Candace wanted to crawl in a hole and die. To her that call proved she wasn't even successful as a mother. When a friend laughingly said something to her about their needing to go on a diet together, Candace took it personally. Any other time, when Candace wasn't depressed, she would have laughed with her friend. As it was, the least little thing added to the depth of her depression.

For women like Candace, this phenomenon may be due to a depressed woman's lessened ability to cope and be flexible; her actions are not what they should be. Or the phenomena could occur on an unconscious level; the depressed woman unconsciously sets herself up to prove how awful she is or how bad her situation is. Either way, the result is unnecessary and often hard-to-forget emotional pain.

Depression intensifies a woman's sense of helplessness. If you are depressed due to learned helplessness, a failure to fight the illness contributes to your sense of helplessness. Unconsciously you may see your depression as one more thing over which you have no control.

Depression contributes to physical illnesses. A lingering or serious depression may make you more vulnerable to disease. It weakens your immune system.

Depression leads to hopelessness and possible suicide. If you are depressed, all you can remember are moments of suffering; the good moments are blotted out. This would be bearable if you had the conviction that things would eventually improve. But hopelessness makes you think things never will improve. Your suffering is unbearable and appears unending; you may erroneously conclude that suicide is your only way of escape. The earlier you fight the illness, the sooner you will begin to feel better. As with other illnesses, the longer you wait before treating it, the more difficult it can be to treat.[1]

Depression experts talk in terms of a kindling effect.[2] An initial episode of depression appears in response to a severe stressful event. The next time, the event doesn't have to be quite as severe to ignite a depressive episode. As time goes on, it takes less and less to send the sufferer into an emotional tailspin. Fighting depression thwarts its power for recurrence.

Depression is a powerful enemy we should never underestimate.

Fortunately, many weapons are available for fighting this illness. Some of those weapons are stored in our arsenal, others are available through professionals.

WHAT CAN A WOMAN DO FOR HERSELF?

Accept responsibility. A woman will be more successful in overcoming depression if she admits, "Depression is *my* problem."

You may have a genetic predisposition for depression, you may have been unloved as a child, you may have been rejected or fired, but that's beside the point. As long as you blame others or blame your past, you'll be a victim rather than a victor over depression.

Many of us hate to admit we're depressed because it's not a respectable illness. We would much rather admit to having a physical illness or having too much stress in our lives.

When I was depressed, I felt all my influence as a Christian would crumble the minute people learned I was depressed. I valued the opinion of my fellow Christians, particularly the women in the Sunday school class I taught. I was afraid they would think less of me as a teacher and as a person. The night I confessed my struggle with depression (at the Sunday school class meeting where we exchanged "war stories") was a big step for me, but not big enough.

Once I confessed to the class, I was certain I would never be depressed again. I assumed being conscious of the illness would be enough to prevent its recurrence. But the enemy called depression is very clever. When he came back a year later, I didn't recognize him. He was dressed in different clothing.

This time I was certain I had a serious physical illness. When I described my symptoms to my doctor over the phone, he implied that I might be depressed. When I resisted the idea, he asked me to come see him. Before my appointment, I stayed awake all night developing arguments on why I was not depressed. The fact that I couldn't sleep should have been a strong clue that I was. The next day, the doctor listened to all my arguments. He even let me describe all the possible physical ailments I thought I had. Then he said, "You are depressed, and your denial is a classic symptom."

"If I am depressed, then I'm in trouble."

"What do you mean?"

I had studied enough about depression to know that recurring episodes mean a person needs help. I told the doctor about being depressed before, something he didn't know.

My confession to the Sunday school class had not been an admission of responsibility, it was a report of how I had been a powerless victim of circumstances. Talking with the doctor forced me to admit I had a problem. A famous psychologist once said, "If you can own the mess you're in, there is hope for you and help available. As long as you blame others, you will be a victim for the rest of your life."[3] Admitting I had a problem ignited a resolve in me to fight depression. That was an important step because depression requires commitment.

Commit to win. When Jesus stopped by the pool of Siloam in Jerusalem, He asked the lame man, "Do you want to get well?" (John 5:6). That's a question every depressed woman needs to ask herself because she must *want* to get well if she is going to win against depression.

It's easy to become discouraged in your battle. Things that ordinarily wouldn't bother you become devastating events that impede progress. You need to realize that setbacks are normal. Some battles may be lost, but the war can be won. You also need to realize that depression's grip is very strong. The nature of the illness makes some women want to hold onto it like an old bathrobe or a favorite pair of tennis shoes.

One reason some of us may unconsciously hold onto depression is because it can be power. If we feel helpless, our sadness may be a way of trying to get family members to change. "Don't you see what you're doing to me? Can't you see how I'm suffering?" Depression can be a way of keeping injustices or hurts alive. One woman who became depressed after being fired from two jobs within a year said, "I kept waiting for the world to come to its senses, call, and apologize." One woman who lost her six-year-old son in tragic, freakish circumstances was depressed for four years. She told me, "As long as I was depressed, Sonny was alive."

We must want to get well so much that we stay in the war in spite of discouragement and defeat. We must be willing to let go of the past and surrender any power that depression offers. Winning the war against depression requires moving forward.

Analyze the trigger. Even though I can't always keep the black cloud of depression from hovering, I've found I can fight to keep it from staying. My offensive position is more effective and efficient if I know why the cloud has appeared. I have a better view of what I am fighting, and I can see how to fight it.

To figure out why I'm depressed, I turn the triggers listed in chapter 5 into questions.

+ What stressful event has recently occurred in my life?
+ What have I lost?
+ How long have I felt this way?
+ How heavy is my load?
+ What did I expect of others? Of myself?
+ Have I failed?
+ Have I lost sight of God's purpose for my life?
+ Do I feel helpless or trapped?
+ Have I been rejected?
+ Am I holding back grief, guilt, or anger?

If the black cloud of depression rolls in because your load is too heavy, then your weapon of choice may be taking time out. You wouldn't expect to jog two miles a day on a broken leg. You would stay off your feet for a while and take it easy. Depression may be your body's way of saying, "Time out. I need to recover." A brief time out from responsibilities or a slowing down of activity may be beneficial. When God responded to Elijah's depression, He started at his most basic level of need with food and rest (1 Kings 19:5-8).

If you're depressed because you're holding back grief, guilt, or anger, you need to find appropriate ways to express those emotions. If unrealistic expectations of yourself or others have caused your depression, you may have to find ways to change your expectations. Knowing why you are depressed can help you select your weapons for fighting.

Evaluate the severity. If your symptoms are mild, you may want to fight depression with self-help techniques (chapters 12 and 13). If you are severely depressed, you will probably not be able to determine why you are depressed. Your illness prevents you from doing that kind of analyzing, or the reasons could be buried so deeply that you can't find them. You will want to engage the help of professionals trained to fight depression (chapter 14).

A moderately depressed woman may want to use self-help techniques or professional help or both. If she knows why she is depressed and is able to carry on her daily routines, self-help techniques may be the right weapons for her. If she doesn't know why she is depressed and her functioning at work or home is impaired, she will need professional help to wage her war successfully.

Once a woman is ready to fight her depression and she has done some analyzing of what triggered it and evaluated its severity, she's ready to take action.

Chapter Twelve

Helping Yourself Through Action

~

Why is action so important in fighting depression? "If you do nothing, you will become preoccupied with the flood of negative,
destructive thoughts. If you do something, you will be temporarily distracted from that internal dialogue of self-denigration."[1] Effort brings
relief and sparks hope. The inner room created by the distraction fills
with hope.

Dr. David Burns writes that just about any meaningful activity has
a decent chance of brightening a person's mood.[2] Here are a few suggestions to fight depression.

FIND SOMEONE TO TALK TO

Talking externalizes the problem. Your depression may look altogether
different or seem more manageable when you bring it out in the open.

Talking with someone brings emotional relief. It provides more energy
to fight depression and paves the way for the development of insight
and positive action.

Talking ends the pretense. Most of us occasionally "cut and paste"
ourselves together to do our jobs, to teach a Bible study, or to chair the
church's nominating committee. We don't always feel like doing these
things, but we do them anyway, putting on a brave front. Likewise,
many of us are tempted to do that with depression, giving the world
the impression we are handling life just fine. That approach intensifies
depression. Talking with someone diminishes the intensity.

Talking engages the help and prayerful support of others. It takes away the loneliness of bearing the problem alone. For very good reasons, the Bible says, "Confess your faults one to another, and pray one for another, that ye may be healed" (James 5:16, KJV).

Be selective with whom you talk. You don't want to talk with someone who has simplistic answers to all of life's difficulties or continuously interrupts with her own experiences. You don't want to talk with someone who sees depression as some sort of moral failure. Talking with the wrong person may make you more depressed!

Talk with someone who understands the struggle that accompanies depression, who is a good listener, who can keep confidences, who will not be shocked or judgmental, and who is not equipped with ready answers. Those who make the best listeners are usually people who have experienced deep sorrow in life and have recovered.

Once you find a nonjudgmental listener, you might approach her by saying: "I'm having difficulty. I believe I am depressed, and I need a listening ear. May I talk with you sometime? I would need about an hour of your time." With this kind of approach, the listener knows exactly what is expected of her. By mentioning the time, both of you have an exit to the conversation when it occurs. Talking about depression can be tiring for both the speaker and the listener.

Staying within the time frame will be difficult for many depressed women. Some of us wait too long to talk. When we finally get a good listener, an hour seems like five minutes, but it doesn't to the listener. After an hour, if you need to talk more, you might say, "I really appreciate your time today. It's been helpful. Would it be all right if we got together again sometime? Perhaps an hour next week."

If you continually find yourself needing to go back to the same listener, consider seeing a mental health professional (chapters 14 and 16). You may not want to get well and are using your listener as a ruminating partner.

FIND ACTIVITIES TO DISTRACT YOUR MIND

To successfully distract your mind, you must become so involved in an activity that your mind shifts focus. The goal is to shift from negative, destructive thoughts so that your mind experiences relief from depression. Distraction can often be achieved through involvement with people. A woman already involved in small groups and with family and friends will want to maintain those relationships during her fight with depression. People with many friends and relatives tend to have less difficulty recovering from depression than those with few social supports.[3]

Being with others also gives us an opportunity to square our perceptions and thoughts against reality. Others can offer us a different perspective. Stella found herself with few social supports when her children left home. She had been so involved in their lives that she hadn't noticed how few friends she had. When depression hit, she had little support. In an effort to make some friends, Stella joined a Bible study group. The study was very controlled; the leader lectured and the members took notes. When the leader lectured, Stella often found her attention drawn to her troubles. "Nobody cares for me. All of these women have friends but me."

After four weeks, Stella mustered up the courage to try a mission action group in her church. This group did a variety of activities, including rolling bandages, making soup for the homeless, and visiting nursing homes. A lot of easy conversation took place while rolling bandages and chopping carrots for the soup. At the nursing homes, Stella focused on the needs of the residents and tried to cheer them up. With each group activity, Stella found her depression diminished until it finally lifted. In the process, she also made some new friends who would be available if she ever became depressed again.

EXERCISE

Depression is an illness of passivity. As one woman said, "I simply wanted to lie [there] without moving until my body rotted." Exercise fights the passivity as Newton's law of physics suggests: "A body at rest tends to stay at rest; a body in motion tends to stay in motion."

Exercise also affects brain chemistry. Regular aerobic exercise (such as running, biking, or swimming) can ease mild and some moderate cases of depression by raising the level of certain brain chemicals— some of the same brain chemicals that are affected by antidepressants. Even a brisk midday walk for ten to twenty minutes can help. It can energize, cut tension, and increase optimism.

For greater effectiveness, you should exercise regularly at least three times a week (five or more is better) for at least half an hour each time. A combination of walking and running is a good way to start, since no equipment is necessary, and can be done either alone or in a group.

LISTEN TO MUSIC

One magazine article on beating mild depression began with these words: "Don't wallow in a foul mood. Run for the gym, and take your headphones."

When King Saul experienced prolonged periods of depression, his servants brought a young shepherd named David to play his harp for the king. David's music seemed to soothe Saul's melancholy moods, and he quickly became a court favorite (1 Samuel 16:14-23).

Harp music is known for its soothing qualities. That's one way music can be a weapon against depression; the right kind of music can soothe and comfort.

Music is effective against depression in other ways as well. The lyrics or message of a song can be a distraction from ruminating. Moving to the rhythm of music can release tension and break up immobilizing feelings of depression.

LIST YOUR CHOICES

When Naomi and Ruth returned to Bethlehem, they were destitute widows. Naomi's mood of depression and bitterness reflected her hopelessness. In an effort to provide for them, Ruth gleaned in the fields. When she returned from gleaning, Ruth told Naomi about meeting Boaz, the kind owner of the fields who noticed her (Ruth 2:17-19). Then Naomi's mood brightened (2:22) because she could see a solution to their poverty—Boaz. He was a relative who could redeem their situation. Naomi advised Ruth on how to approach him about being their redeemer by marrying Ruth.

Seeing possibilities raises hope. If you are depressed, like Naomi you may think you have no choices, but you do. Take a pencil and paper and list your choices, even those you don't like or that seem bizarre. Friends, family members, or professionals may add insight for the woman too close to the situation to see clearly.

Once you make the list, decide which one to follow. Making a choice and following through provides you a route for recovery.

ACT "AS IF"

External changes in behavior often precede, rather than follow, internal change. If a woman acts the way she wishes she felt, instead of the way she feels, her feelings may change. For example, Freeda had been depressed for four weeks when her boss asked her to make a product presentation to some business people from out of town. Fearful of jeopardizing her job, she decided to put on a false front. During the presentation, Freeda smiled, joked, and played the part of a happy, confident person. To her delight, when she arrived home that night, she discovered her depression had lightened considerably. Acting as if she were happy changed the way she felt.

INVEST IN YOURSELF

Some depressed women are so busy they don't have time to invest in themselves. They continually give and give to other people until they give out. Others live with people who denigrate them continuously. What these women need are some deposits in their emotional banks. They may have to be the ones to make those deposits.

One way you can make deposits in your emotional bank is by doing something nice for yourself like taking a nice long bath, watching a funny movie, or spending some time by water. One woman who was depressed when her fortieth birthday came around in the middle of January decided on swimming in a heated pool as a gift to herself. She called a local motel with an indoor pool. They said that while they usually only opened their pool to motel guests or those who had a monthly membership, since it was her birthday, they would make an exception. For six dollars, she spent a pleasant afternoon going between the pool and the whirlpool, lazily watching the snow fall on the glass roof. The experience rejuvenated her.

Some women may feel uncomfortable about making an investment in themselves. They are accustomed to putting others first, but their depression may be saying to them, "Your energy is depleted. You need to invest in yourself."

INVEST IN OTHERS

An interesting line in the book of Job is, "And the LORD turned the captivity of Job, when he prayed for his friends . . ." (Job 42:10, KJV). A woman's captivity to depressive, self-destructive thoughts can turn, too, when the center of her attention is drawn away from herself and directed toward others. It can change her internal conversation from, "I am not good for anything," to "I am useful to someone; I can do something effectively." One woman who battles depression volunteered for the church ministry to homebound people. She told me, "I always feel better when I can go and see people who are a bit worse off than myself, especially when they show courage over the circumstances in their lives. Visiting others switches my thoughts from negative ones to positive ones."

Another woman calls a friend down the street with three preschoolers and says, "May I have your kids for an hour or two?" This gives the friend a break and gives her a chance to get involved in some kid chatter filled with wonder and questions. She takes them to the large school parking lot near her house where they fly kites. As the kites soar into the air, her mood lifts.

Our chances for winning against depression are greater if we use a variety of methods to fight it. These eight suggestions are but a few; others may be found in books and articles on depression. You can come up with your own ideas by asking:

1. What can I do to change my passive, helpless behavior?
2. What can I do to change my sad emotions?
3. What can I do to change my thinking?
4. What can I do to change my feelings about myself?

The weapons a woman chooses to fight with are not as important as the fact that she fights.

Chapter Thirteen

Lord, I Need Your Help . . .

~

God wants to help women who are depressed. Some women, though, may be reluctant to seek God's help. Some feel unworthy; others wrestle with guilt—both real and imagined, which hinders them from approaching Him. Some may be reluctant to seek God because He disappointed them. The stressful events that triggered their depressions were never supposed to happen to "good people." Still reeling from disappointment, they are afraid to trust God again. As one woman wrote in her journal, "I feel forsaken by God almost to the point that I think He enjoys seeing me in pain. I'm afraid to trust Him again." Yet they also desperately long for God's help. Battling depression is tough and lonely; they could use His strength and His companionship.

God wants to help us. He wants to offer His strength and companionship, but He needs a channel through which to work. If you really want to get well, you can offer God direct access through prayer, praise, or journaling.

FOCUSED, VERBAL PRAYER

The prayer, "Oh, God, help me feel better," is too general to do the depressed woman much good. Usually a prayer like this is a thought prayer. Repeated over and over, it stokes pessimistic ruminations. Besides, it's so general it would be hard to recognize an answer. Its desperate tone contributes to a woman's feelings of helplessness. (We hear our prayers as well as God!)

If you want God's help through prayer, I recommend that your prayers be focused and verbal. Focus on God's realness. Imagine Jesus' presence—across the table, at the opposite end of the couch, in a nearby chair. Jesus is real, He is present, so imagining His physical presence is appropriate. If you are depressed your spiritual vision is blocked and your ability to concentrate diminished. You can use your God-given imagination to acknowledge Jesus' presence.

Praying aloud also acknowledges His presence. When you pray aloud, you are talking to someone who really exists!

Verbal praying also helps you present your needs and be more in control of your prayer. (Thought prayers make it easy to drift in and out of prayer.) Voicing your requests lessens your timidity and assures you that you have, indeed, presented your needs to someone who can help.

You will feel freer to pray out loud and focus on Jesus' realness when you pray conversationally. "Jesus, I'm glad You are here with me. I need a good listener, someone to understand what I'm going through. I know You do. You were rejected by Your friends, and there was even a time when You felt abandoned by God. That's the way I'm feeling. I need Your help." With this introduction, you can proceed to tell Jesus about your situation the same way you'd talk with a trusted friend.

PRAYING FOR INSIGHT

Prayer is a spiritual weapon you might want to use in addition to self-help techniques (chapters 11 and 12) or in addition to professional help (chapter 14).

For example, you might want to use prayer to help you discover why you are depressed. "Dear Jesus, light of the world, I need your light to shine upon my situation so I can see it clearly. Show me why I am depressed." You may want to use prayer when you have a hard time listing the choices or alternatives before you. "Lord Jesus, help me see the alternatives in my situation. Here's what my situation is . . . (describe situation). I'm lost as to what I can do. Please show me some alternatives and give me the courage to choose one."

When my doctor diagnosed my depression, he recommended antidepressants or psychiatric help or both. I chose to see a psychiatrist. The psychiatrist was extremely helpful, but because my depression was so strongly tied in to my spiritual life, I don't think I could have recovered completely without prayer.

In between sessions with the psychiatrist, my recovery was hampered by what I referred to as the "four o'clock blues." The gain made with the psychiatrist got eroded by small things that triggered unpleasant memories of the bizarre things that had happened. Confusion would roll in and the bleak sadness of depression would converge on me, especially late in the afternoon. I needed to find a way to deal with these "four o'clock blues" if I was going to overcome my depression.

The answer for me was honest praying. Each time the four o'clock blues hit, I let the tears flow and unleashed my anger and hurt. "God, how could You do this to us? How could You let us hurt when we've tried so hard to serve You?" I told God all that I was feeling until my emotion was spent. Then God seemed closer and new strength filled me.

Honest prayer opened the way for God to come in and do a work of grace. Honest prayer gave God a channel through which He could help me.

PRAYER THERAPY

Even when my physical and emotional symptoms were gone, I seemed stuck in a holding pattern—unwilling to move forward into the future. I did not believe God had a purpose for my life. I had to find a way to believe that once again if I was going to be completely well. I used prayer therapy to do this.

Prayer therapy is outlined by Dr. William R. Parker and Elaine St. Johns in *Prayer Can Change Your Life*. It involves surrender and affirmation. In surrender (or release, as I like to call it), we give God all the rubbish within us. We give Him our fears, our guilt, our anger, our grief, our broken dreams, and our faulty assumptions. As the Bible says, "Casting all your care upon him, for he cares for you" (1 Peter 5:7, NKJV). The surrender (or release) creates an inner void. The void must not fill up again with the same rubbish we released. The void must be filled with positive, affirmative prayer.

In affirmative prayer, we put helpful, creative thoughts into that void. We affirm ourselves free of the rubbish we release, and we affirm the kind of person we want to be or the kind of things we want to replace the rubbish. In releasing, I prayed, "Lord, I give You my hurts and my grief and my despair. I forgive the people whom I believed hurt me. I give You the past. I release it to You."

In affirmation, I prayed, "Today, Lord, I see myself as being free of depression and free of hurt. I see myself as feeling good about life again. I see You as smiling in approval of me because I remained faithful without understanding what was happening. I affirm my trust in You. I believe You have a purpose behind all that has happened. I'm hopeful about the future."

The first morning I prayed this way, the effect of it lasted about one hour. Then I was back to wallowing in self-pity. The next morning, I prayed again in the same way. This time, the effect lasted longer. Eventually, through surrender and affirmation, the day came when I was free and believed once again in my purpose before God.

PRAISE BRINGS HEALING

To praise God is to relinquish preoccupation with self, something that is characteristic of many depressions. As we give up control, God comes in and imparts His strength. As the Bible says, God inhabits the praises of His people (Psalm 22:3, KJV). Whenever God is adored, reverenced, and worshiped, He openly manifests Himself.

It's not easy to praise God when we are depressed. In fact, praising God is probably the most difficult self-help technique listed in chapters 12 and 13. It is truly a "sacrifice of praise" (Hebrews 13:15). To praise God while depressed is a sacrifice because it requires an action contrary to everything we are feeling. We must sacrifice our own judgment, our own opinion, and our own evaluation of our situation. We must sacrifice all the attention we've been giving to self and give it to God.

The writer of Hebrews gives two helpful tips in making this sacrifice. He refers to the sacrifice of praise as "the fruit of our lips," and he makes that synonymous with "giving thanks to his name" (Hebrews 13:15, NKJV). "The fruit of our lips" means that the sacrifice of praise is verbal. Practically speaking, the praise must be said out loud as if we mean it.

Because we don't feel like praising God when we're depressed, we're going to be short on words. "Giving thanks to His name" is a good way to initiate verbal praise. You can begin simply. "Thank You, Lord, that

I can voice thanks to You. Thank You, Lord, that I have shelter. Thank You, Lord, that I am alive. Thank You, that I have hands to reach up to You. Thank You, Lord. . . ." The discipline of giving thanks will lead to praise. As we verbally praise God, we reinforce our belief in Him, gain strength from the knowledge of who He is, and give Him a channel to respond to us.

JOURNALING

Journal writing provides several benefits.

Writing in a journal can nail down what has to be done. One woman wrote, "I have to write about what happened to me to survive. Writing will help me be deliberate in my determination to get through this depression. Writing will help me pray deliberately and specifically. Without writing prayers, they become cries of 'Why, Why?'"

Writing in a journal can be an emotional release. As one woman explained, "During a long hospitalization for deep depression, a journal was the only thing I could relate to. I wrote, almost nonstop for days. It is the most valuable writing I have ever done. The process of all that 'stuff' pouring out was clearing and cathartic. . . . When I had poured out all I needed to, I felt very relieved and much better."[1]

We can record what we're thinking and feeling. We may want to describe the stresses in our lives. We may want to write our prayers and our praises. The journal can also help us plan a strategy for getting over depression. It can be a place for recording strengthening quotes and Bible verses. Writing out a verse helps us to concentrate on it and absorb it.

Writing in a journal can help us untangle and organize our thoughts. Writing helps us make sense out of what we're thinking. There's no need to worry about grammar, punctuation, and organization of material. What's written doesn't have to make sense. Thoughts and feelings are expressed where no one else can see them or criticize them.

Journaling can be done on bits of paper here and there, but is usually done in a notebook. The first page can begin with, "I'm . . . (name), my address is. . . . Today (list date), I'm beginning a journal to help me with the war I'm having with depression. I first noticed being depressed. . . ."

You don't have to make journal entries every day, but in fighting depression, you need to make them frequently. Dating the entries will enable you to look back and see progress. Then you can make an invest-ment in your self by noting how proud you are of your progress. You can congratulate yourself for what you're achieving. Two cautions about journaling your depression: (1) The journal shouldn't become a tool for keeping a list of wrongs or of how awful life is or of how bad the situ-ation is. This kind of listing fuels depression. (2) Journal entries can contribute to pessimistic ruminating. You shouldn't worry about that when you're getting started. But after a couple of weeks, you should experience some relief. Don't cover the same ground over and over. If you do, journaling will not help.

On the whole, journaling is an effective weapon for a woman to use to open herself to God's help. Like prayer and praise, it gives God a channel to help us win against depression. As we use these tools, a time will come when we will be able to say to God, "You turned my wailing into dancing; you removed my sackcloth and clothed me with joy" (Psalm 30:11).

Chapter Fourteen

Do You Need Professional Help?

 ~~~

The day Anna dropped the scrambled eggs she decided she needed help to fight her depression.

After putting off getting up, Anna tried to get the children's breakfast ready before the school bus arrived. So groggy that she didn't realize what she was doing, she picked up the iron skillet without a pot holder and immediately dropped it. "Oh, how could I have done such a thing? Look, I've wasted all those eggs. What will the children do without their breakfast? How could I have been so clumsy? Just look at the mess I made."

Anna's husband heard her self-tirade and walked over to gently but firmly grasp her shoulders. "Anna," he said, "get a grip on yourself. They're only eggs. The children will survive. It's not the end of the world. I'll clean up the eggs, and you get out the cereal for the children."

After the children were out the door, he said, "You've made a valiant effort to fight your depression. You joined that exercise group at church, yet you came home each time exhausted. I've noticed you writing in your journal, and in the night I've heard you praying for God's help. But the depression has gone on too long. You deserve to feel better. Won't you consider getting professional help?"

When he left for work, Anna looked up the number of a psychiatrist who was a member of their church. Her hand shook as she dialed the number, but she knew it was the right thing to do.

A depressed woman needs professional help if:

◆ She doesn't know what caused her depression. The black cloud of despair hovering over her came out of nowhere and feels dark and deep, and seemingly without a cause.

◆ She is having suicidal thoughts.

◆ She is having delusional thoughts or hallucinating.

◆ She can't sleep, or is losing a serious amount of weight or experiencing severe physical discomfort that affects her health.

◆ She's had repeated depressive episodes.

◆ The depression is hurting her marriage, family, or job.

◆ Her depression has lasted longer than one year.

◆ Her depression is so intense that self-help techniques bring no relief.

What professional help options are there?

Depression can be diagnosed and treated by psychiatrists, psychologists, clinical social workers, family therapists, psychiatric nurse specialists, counselors, and other mental health professionals, as well as by primary care physicians. The laws that govern these professions vary, but general guidelines are given here:

Psychiatrists are medical doctors skilled and practiced in the treatment of depressive disorders. Their job is to delineate between the various types and causes of depression. They can prescribe medications and admit patients and treat them in hospitals.

A *psychologist* holds a degree in psychology, an academic discipline dealing with the study of mental processes and behavior. Clinical psychologists generally hold a doctoral degree in psychology.

Clinical social workers have usually taken a two-year graduate program, including fieldwork, to obtain a master's degree in social work.

Marital and family therapists generally have a master's degree in marriage, family, and child counseling.

Psychiatric nurse specialists are registered nurses who have specialized training in treating mental or psychiatric disorders.

Clinical mental health counselors have earned at least a master's degree. Plus they've had several years of supervised experience in a clinical setting.

In addition, there's a wide range of other professionals who can help people with depression, including pastors and counselors on church staffs. Of the mental health professionals listed here, only psychiatrists may prescribe medicine for depression.

TAKING THE FIRST STEP

The first professional a depressed woman may want to contact is her personal physician for a thorough medical examination. Fatigue, disturbed sleep, or other symptoms may have a physical origin, so a good medical examination is in order.

If you're taking this first step, you need to tell your physician what medicines you currently use, because some medicines cause depression. And you need to say explicitly that you think you're depressed. Nonpsychiatrist physicians spot major depression less frequently than mental health professionals do.

If your physician diagnoses your condition as depression, he or she can treat you with antidepressants. Or you may want to seek the help of a mental health professional. With the exception of psychiatrists, mental health professionals do not prescribe medicine. They have a variety of ways of treating depression, particularly through psychotherapy (sometimes called talk therapy).

You may want to see both your physician and a mental health professional to receive medicine and psychotherapy.

If your depression is severe, you may need electroconvulsive therapy. In that case, you will need a psychiatrist's help.

The major types of treatment for depression are psychotherapy, antidepressants, and electroconvulsive therapy.

WHAT PSYCHOTHERAPY OFFERS

In a psychotherapy session, the depressed patient or client talks to a trained mental health professional. She discusses her problems, expressing any hostility, fear, guilt, and other emotions with freedom. The therapist listens, probes, responds, and educates.

Talking with a psychotherapist is not the same as talking to a friend or spouse. Psychotherapy refers to "the work of a professional—someone who is specially trained and employed in using a knowledge of human interaction to help people solve emotional or other problems."[1] Because I write and speak about depression, some people assume I can be a therapist. I cannot. While I know about depression and am a good listener, I cannot lead people through the process of recovery. Psychotherapy is more than listening.

Some therapies emphasize insight. Through therapy, you can make sense out of your confusion, gaining insight about yourself and your situation. You can identify and label your feelings and learn why you feel the way you do.

Some therapies delve into the person's past, exploring the unconscious motivations behind feelings. Other therapies focus on the present and the future to help you learn better ways to deal with the stressful events that have triggered your depression and gain skills for moving into the future.

Therapies that help you recognize your response style and cognitive distortions reveal how your thinking patterns affect your moods and how you can change those thinking patterns.

Some therapies primarily educate. You can learn what depression is and why you are depressed. You can learn how to function more successfully and how to handle stress.

Therapies that offer encouragement and support on a regular basis emphasize how to cope with the illness and with life.

If you choose psychotherapy, you will see your therapist at least once a week for sessions of thirty, forty, or fifty minutes. The number of sessions usually ranges from six to thirty, depending on the kind of therapy. Several sessions are needed before noticeable improvement.

Therapy's effectiveness depends upon these three things: (1) the therapist's skill and experience, (2) how well the patient and therapist work together, and (3) the patient's motivation and commitment to work. While therapy sounds simple, it involves hard work. Effort, commitment, and persistence are the keys to success. If you are hopeful, cooperative, and committed, you have a better chance of successful treatment.

More than half of the patients with mild to moderate forms of major depression respond well to psychotherapy.[2] Psychotherapy alone is not recommended as the only treatment for severe depression or for bipolar disorders. Both of these conditions need medication.

WHY TAKE ANTIDEPRESSANTS?

Antidepressants are medications that target the biological basis of depression. They are linked to neurotransmitters in the brain.

Each nerve cell in the brain is separated by tiny gaps. The neurotransmitters carry messages across these gaps to a receptor.

Each neurotransmitter has a special shape that helps it fit exactly into a corresponding receptor like a key in an ignition switch. When the neurotransmitter "key" is inserted into its matching receptor's "ignition," the cell fires and sends the message on its way. Once the message is sent, the neurotransmitter is either absorbed into the cell or burned up by enzymes patrolling the gaps.[3]

While there are as many as 100 kinds of neurotransmitters, three appear to have a particular connection to depression. They are norepinephrine, serotonin, and dopamine. "The pathways for these neurotransmitters reach deep into many of the parts of the brain responsible for functions that are affected in depression—sleep, appetite, mood, and sexual interest."[4]

What possible kinds of situations occur with the neurotransmitters to cause depression?

1. *Low levels of norepinephrine, serotonin, and dopamine.* When the levels are low, messages can't get across the gaps, and communication in the brain slows down. Medications that boost levels of these neurotransmitters also ease depression.[5]

2. *A neurotransmitter can't fit into its receptor for some reason.*[6] If that happens, the nerve cell can't get the message it's supposed to send to some part of the body.

3. *The neurotransmitters affected by antidepressants could affect yet another—yet to be identified—neurotransmitter that's even more directly involved in depression.*[7] Antidepressants can raise neurotransmitter levels almost immediately, but the depression doesn't lift until weeks after drug therapy begins. Perhaps raising the levels affects another neurotransmitter more directly related to depression.

Antidepressants alter these situations. They improve mood, sleep, energy levels, and concentration. They do not make a person "high" the way marijuana or cocaine might. If a person who is not depressed takes antidepressants, the medication won't do anything for her.

Antidepressants and tranquilizers are not the same thing. They act on different parts of the brain. Tranquilizers, such as Valium, Librium, Miltown, and Xanax are really depressants of the central nervous system. Taking tranquilizers for depression may intensify the problem.

Antidepressants are available through prescription and, in general, only physicians can write prescriptions. This doesn't mean a woman who wants to take antidepressants shouldn't go to mental health professionals other than psychiatrists for treatment. Mental health professionals usually work in tandem with psychiatrists who provide prescriptions for antidepressants when they are needed.

WHAT ELECTROCONVULSIVE THERAPY OFFERS

Severely depressed people who haven't responded to any other treatment may benefit from electroconvulsive therapy. Electroconvulsive therapy (ECT) is a series of brief electrical stimulations of that part of the brain which mediates basic biological functions such as sleep, appetite, energy, and sex. The electrical stimulations restore the severely depressed person's biological functions to normal.

In ECT treatment, a small amount of electrical current is sent through the brain for one to two seconds. The patient experiences a brain seizure lasting about 40 seconds.[8] ECT is administered *after* the patient is put to sleep with a short-acting anesthetic and *after* the patient's muscles are relaxed so that muscle contractions from the treatment will not damage muscles or bones. Patients do not remember or feel the treatment.[9] Treatment usually consists of six to twelve seizures over two to four weeks. The series of seizures bring about the improvement.

The notion of passing electricity through the brain is frightening to many people. There were abuses of ECT early in its history when it was known as shock therapy. Wild tales were told and horror scenes were dramatized in the movies. Modern ECT can provide a safe, quick recovery for severely depressed people.

In the experience and judgment of many physicians (and patients with severe depressions who have received ECT and other antidepressant treatments), electroconvulsive or "shock" therapy is the single most effective treatment for severe depression and has a number of advantages over other treatments.[10]

Here are the benefits of ECT as treatment for severe depression. It has been found that ECT:

- ◆ Works rapidly so that patients can quickly return to productive living[11]
- ◆ Has a higher success rate for severe depression than any other single treatment approach[12]
- ◆ Is more side-effect-free than many antidepressants[13]
- ◆ Is the treatment of choice when a person is making dangerous suicide attempts[14]
- ◆ Is necessary when a patient is in poor medical condition[15]
- ◆ Works when other therapies aren't successful in treating severe depression[16]

One therapist who became depressed (yes, even mental health professionals get depressed) found no combination of therapy and medication to relieve her depression. Martha wrote in her journal, "All escapes are illusory—distractions, sleep, drugs, doctors, answers, hope." Only a series of electroconvulsive therapy treatments administered over time in an inpatient setting brought Martha back from the edge of death. ECT has helped many acutely suffering and often suicidally depressed people. "As many as 100,000 people receive ECT each year."[17]

ECT does have some side effects, as all medical treatments of depression do. One major side effect is ". . . transient confusion right after each treatment. Other immediate side effects are nausea, headaches, or muscle soreness. Some patients experience some memory loss, but it usually lasts for no longer than a month."[18]

If you want more information about ECT, check with a psychiatrist or look for general books on depression that take a comprehensive medical approach.

HOSPITALIZATION

Early treatment of depression can prevent the need for hospitalization. "Most people can be safely treated for depression outside a hospital setting, particularly if they have friends or family to provide physical and emotional support. However, a short stay—typically less than a month—in either a psychiatric hospital or a psychiatric unit of a general hospital may be necessary in some cases."[19]

Hospitalization should be considered if a depressed person is threatening to kill herself or others, if she is so apathetic that she can't feed herself, if there's evidence of severe agitation or psychosis, or there is a dangerous concurrent medical condition. For example, she may have severe diabetes, but because she is depressed, she's not following prescribed treatment. She needs to be in a hospital where treatment for both the medical condition and the depression can be monitored.

PURSUING THE OPTIONS

Psychotherapy, antidepressants, a combination of psychotherapy and antidepressants, electroconvulsive therapy, and hospitalization are effective means of treating depression. Even with these various treatment options available, only one in three depressed people seeks help.[20]

Perhaps the most important thing family and friends can do for a woman who is depressed is to encourage her to get help. Many of us suffer silently, too uninformed to reach for the help that is available. Not knowing what to expect would make a person reluctant to use antidepressants or participate in psychotherapy, so the next two chapters provide additional information about these treatments.

Chapter Fifteen

Making Sense of Antidepressants

When God's people were perched at the edge of the Promised Land, Moses, their leader, sent spies to explore the area and report what the land and its inhabitants were like (Numbers 13). The spies came back with conflicting reports.

Similarly, the depressed woman is perched at the edge of the Land of Antidepressants, wondering if she should enter. Others have, and, like Moses' spies, returned with conflicting reports:

✦ "I feel normal now. It's as if I had been driving a car for years with the parking brake on. Now it's off."
✦ "I'll never take another antidepressant. The side effects are intolerable."

Before a woman can decide which, if any, antidepressant might be helpful for her, she needs information. That's the purpose of this chapter.

Cyclic Antidepressants

The classes of antidepressants are determined by the chemistry of the drugs and by their effect on the brain. Chemically, *cyclic antidepressants* contain one or more cyclic or ring structures.

Tricyclics were developed first. Tricyclic refers to its three-ring antihistamine chemical structure. A later-developed medication in this class "had four rings and was therefore called 'tetracyclic.' Taken together, the tricyclics and tetracyclics are known as 'heterocyclics' or 'cyclics.'"[1]

Cyclic antidepressants treat depression by raising the level of norepinephrine and serotonin—neurotransmitters that are abnormally low in depressed patients.

But cyclics don't stop with just affecting norepinephrine and serotonin. "They go on to interfere with a range of other neurotransmitter systems and a variety of brain cell receptors, affecting nerve cell communication all over the brain in the process."[2] The more neurotransmitter systems and receptors affected, the more side effects a patient will have.

Among the list of side effects are: tremors, unpleasant taste, dry mouth, nausea, fatigue, weakness, anxiety, diarrhea, headache, sensitivity to sunlight, constipation, indigestion, insomnia, sedation, nervousness, and excessive sweating. (The length of the list does not mean that cyclics are unusually dangerous.)

A person who experiences side effects won't have all of them; she may experience one or two, or none at all. The side effects often disappear quickly or can be reduced by lowering the dosage or changing to another cyclic.

These are some common cyclic antidepressants. The generic names (chemical compounds) are listed first with the trade names given in parentheses.

Amitriptyline (Elavil, Endep, Emitrip, Enovil)
Amoxapine (Asendin)
Clomipramine (Anafranil)
Desipramine (Norpramin, Pertofrane)
Doxepin (Adapin, Sinequan)
Imipramine (Janimine, Tipramine, Tofranil, Tofranil-PM)
Maprotiline (Ludiomil)
Nortriptyline (Pamelor, Aventyl)
Protriptyline (Vivactil)

Monoamine Oxidase Inhibitors (MAOIs)

The neurotransmitters serotonin, norepinephrine, and dopamine are known as monoamines. Once the monoamines "have played their part in sending messages in the brain, they get burned up by a protein in the brain called monoamine oxidase, a liver and brain enzyme."[3] Antidepressants known as monoamine oxidase inhibitors (MAOIs) block this enzyme so the excess neurotransmitters don't get destroyed. They start piling up in the brain and depression lifts.

Unfortunately, MAOIs don't just raise the levels of serotonin, norepinephrine, and dopamine. They also raise another amine called tyramine, a molecule that affects blood pressure. "Large amounts of tyramine may lead to extreme elevations in blood pressure (a hypertensive reaction), sometimes to the point of breaking blood vessels in the brain and causing a stroke or even death."[4]

Aged cheese; sauerkraut; red wine; and aged, smoked, or pickled meats or fish are among the food items that can cause tyramine to flood the brain. Certain medications, when combined with MAOIs, may also cause dangerously high blood pressure or fever and convulsions. Women taking MAOIs should have a complete list of all foods, beverages, and other medications to avoid.

Other side effects include: lightheadedness upon standing, insomnia, delayed orgasm, dry mouth, constipation, and difficult urination.

MAOIs are often prescribed when the depressed person is oversleeping, overeating, and gaining weight rapidly. Some research suggests that, perhaps because they have a stimulating rather than sedating effect, MAOIs may be preferable to cyclic antidepressants for treating dysthymia.[5]

Two common MAOI antidepressants currently available in the United States are Phenelzine (Nardil) and Tranylcypromine (Parnate).

Selective Serotonin Reuptake Inhibitors (SSRIs)

Serotonin, the neurotransmitter that makes people feel calm, is often deficient in depressed people. SSRIs, known as serotonin reuptake inhibitors, tell the brain not to break down serotonin too soon. "*Reuptake* means the body is 'taking up' serotonin and breaking it down. *Inhibitors* slow the action of this reuptake, allowing serotonin to remain at natural levels."[6]

Unlike the scattered approach of cyclic antidepressants or monoamine oxidase inhibitors which interfere with neurotransmitters and receptor sites all over the brain, SSRIs zero in on serotonin. They do not affect other brain systems and consequently, have far less severe side effects than other antidepressants.

What side effects SSRIs have are usually mild and manageable, although once in a while a sensitive person may get a severe reaction. SSRIs may cause nausea, headache, dizziness, dry mouth, insomnia, diarrhea, anxiety, tremor, upper respiratory infection, and a variety of sexual dysfunctions.

Three prominent SSRIs are: Fluoxetine (Prozac), Sertraline (Zoloft), Paroxetine (Paxil).

Most experts agree that no single SSRI is better than the rest, but Prozac is the most well known. It is a very popular antidepressant. When it comes to treating depression, Prozac does have some advantages.

Prozac's half-life is longer. "Half-life" is the time it takes for a drug in the blood to decrease by half of its original dose.[7] Prozac stays in the body much longer than Zoloft, Paxil, and other antidepressants.

This means a woman will be less likely to experience a relapse if she forgets a dose or two of Prozac, and she'll be less likely to have withdrawal effects if she suddenly quits the drug.

If a woman couldn't tolerate taking Prozac, however, she would have to wait longer before trying another antidepressant.

Prozac is not dangerous in high doses. "It's less toxic than other antidepressants and thus harder to overdose on. This factor is important to doctors, since a large proportion of depressives who attempt suicide do so with their own medication. A fatal overdose of Prozac would have to be 100 times a patient's normal daily dose of one pill, compared with only ten times of a tricyclic antidepressant such as Elavil."[8]

The total daily dose of Prozac may be taken as one capsule, making it easier for the depressed person who has a hard time remembering to take her medicine.

Structurally Unrelated Drugs

Bupropion (Wellbutrin), trazodone (Desyrel), venlafaxine (Effexor), and nefazodone (Serzone) are a group of structurally unrelated antidepressants. They don't fit into any of the established antidepressant drug classes of cyclics, MAOIs, or SSRIs. They resulted from scientists fiddling with established antidepressants, looking for medications that are safe, nontoxic, and effective.

Although all four are very effective antidepressants, each one affects different neurotransmitters. While it is not known for sure, the guess is that Wellbutrin affects norepinephrine.[9] Desyrel's complex actions involve both stimulation and blockage of serotonin receptors.[10] Touted as stronger than Prozac, Effexor targets norepinephrine and serotonin.[11] Serzone blocks the serotonin-2A receptors.

The most common side effects shared by Wellbutrin, Effexor, and Desyrel include agitation, dry mouth, insomnia, headache, nausea and vomiting, constipation, and tremors. Serzone may cause less insomnia, less agitation, and less sexual dysfunction than some other antidepressants.

Lithium

Technically not an antidepressant, lithium is a medication that's mostly used for manic depression. It smooths out the hills and valleys of a person's emotional swings. "It can quickly reverse acute mania in 80 percent of people, and stabilize mood in 60 to 70 percent."[12] One woman taking lithium said, "I don't have the highs, I don't have the lows, and I don't miss them."

Lithium can also be effective in the treatment of major depression. It can boost the effectiveness of cyclics, MAOIs, or SSRIs when they don't quite get the job done on their own. "It is also useful as a long-term treatment to prevent recurrences of depressive episodes."[13]

As helpful as it is, lithium treatment is somewhat complicated. A woman can't just take a pill and assume it will work. Lithium works when it reaches the correct level in the bloodstream. Regular blood tests are necessary several times a year to make sure the correct level of the drug is maintained. These tests are not only critical in determining whether the patient is getting enough lithium, but they also guard against getting too much. A slightly high dose can cause weight gain, mental sluggishness, and poor concentration. A very high dose can be fatal.

NONE IS UNIVERSALLY BETTER

While Prozac has received more publicity than the others, no one antidepressant is clearly more effective than the others in treating depression. No antidepressant successfully treats all cases of depression, but they all successfully treat some people. Antidepressants are effective in relieving depression 65 percent[14] to 80 percent[15] of the time.

While each antidepressant has its particular side effects, no one can predict which ones an individual will experience. It's a risk a woman takes when she chooses a recovery route.

Fortunately, there are people to help her.

WORKING WITH A DOCTOR

Since you need a prescription to take an antidepressant, you'll need to work with your doctor and explain your symptoms, medical history, and family history, which offer clues about what medicine is best for you. The doctor will also consider how well you might be expected to tolerate certain side effects.

Finding the right antidepressant and the right dosage may take a while. "Only 50 to 60 percent of patients respond to the first drug they try. A depressed person's doctor may have to prescribe a few antidepressants—not only one from each category, but a couple within a category—before finding the most effective."[16] A doctor may try combining several different drugs. Two antidepressants are sometimes combined to boost their efficiency or to counteract side effects.

Since antidepressant treatment involves complex medical decisions, you may want to seek help from a psychiatrist or a psychopharmacologist instead of your personal doctor. With so many antidepressants currently on the market and more in the process of development, doctors with a general practice may find it hard to stay up on the distinctive of each antidepressant. (A psychiatrist will likely be more specialized in diagnosing the depression and in finding the right medication. A psychopharmacologist is a doctor who specializes in drug treatment.)

WHAT KIND OF TREATMENT CAN I EXPECT?

Acute Treatment. First a doctor will seek to remove the symptoms of depression until you feel well. Most people see benefits in two to six weeks, the time it takes for the antidepressant to reach therapeutic levels.

In this phase, the doctor will want to see you often (possibly every week), in order to check the dosage, discuss side effects, and evaluate the treatment.

Continuation Treatment. After you've felt better for a while, you and your doctor will decide if the depression has ended. Even when it has, you should continue to take the antidepressant medicine for several months. "Research shows that 70 percent of patients become depressed again if they stop taking their antidepressants too early—five weeks or less beyond the point when their symptoms stop. The relapse rate falls to only 14 percent among those who keep taking their antidepressant at least five months after their symptoms abated."[17]

During this phase, you will probably visit your doctor every month or two. After four to nine months, if you continue to feel good, you are declared "recovered" and the medication is gradually tapered off.

Maintenance Treatment. In cases of recurrent depression (three or more episodes) or bipolar depression, a third phase, called maintenance treatment, is used. In maintenance treatment, you stay on medication for a longer period of time. Visits with the doctor are usually scheduled every two to three months. The purpose of this long-term treatment is to prevent recurrence.

The majority of people who take antidepressants are helped. Unless you try them, you will never know if you are part of that majority. Fifty years ago, these drugs weren't even an option. Today drug companies are working hard to find better antidepressants with fewer side effects. Maybe the time will come when there are no conflicting reports from the Land of Antidepressants.

Chapter Sixteen

Four Effective Therapies

~

A report in *U.S. News and World Report* stated that the United States boasts more than 400 kinds of psychotherapy.[1] One book reported 200.[2] Regardless of the correct number, the variety is daunting. With so many different kinds of therapies, how does a person know which to choose? How does a woman who wants to help another woman know which to recommend?

As I researched books and articles on depression for this book, I looked for those therapies most frequently recommended to help those who are depressed. Three particular therapies (and sometimes a combination of two of them) were mentioned over and over. They were behavior therapy, cognitive therapy, and interpersonal therapy. In a national study published in 1989, both cognitive therapy and interpersonal therapy were shown to be just as effective as antidepressants in treating major depression.[3] Behavior therapy is similar to both of them and is often used in conjunction with cognitive therapy.

Dr. Ellen McGrath writes that interpersonal therapy, behavioral therapy, and cognitive therapy are especially valuable treatments because they emphasize action.[4] "All encourage the development, through homework and feedback, of practical skills that enable women to function with greater competence and mastery in their relationships and work lives."[5]

In this chapter, we are going to look at these three therapies plus group therapy. Group therapy can be a critical component of a woman's healing because it meets many of her special needs.[6]

FOCUSING ON THE SYMPTOMS

Behavior therapy is an action-oriented therapy that concentrates on changing behavior. It targets the behavioral symptoms of depression — withdrawal, nonassertiveness, and lack of involvement in pleasurable activities. A behavioral therapist[7] helps the depressed woman recognize her symptoms, eliminate them, and then develop life skills to become more active and powerful in her everyday life.

The therapist often asks the client to monitor her activities, moods and thoughts, sometimes by keeping a written record for a period of time. The written record provides an objective baseline from which to measure change and improvement and gives clues about which activities lift the client's mood and which activities lower it.

Next the therapist may give homework assignments, usually enjoyable activities or social interactions that many depressed people are reluctant to undertake. The tasks may include initiating a conversation, making a phone call, or meeting a friend for lunch.

Most depressed women react negatively to these assignments, saying, "The task is too hard," "I don't think I can do it," "I won't enjoy it." But those who are willing to tackle these activities usually receive positive feedback from their interaction with other people.

Completing the tasks helps:

+ Break the ruminating response
+ Distract patients from their depressive thoughts
+ Disprove their belief that they can't do anything
+ Show them they can help themselves feel better

While working on eliminating the symptoms of depression, the therapist and patient work together to develop life skills that improve her relationships or help her manage the nitty-gritty aspects of life.

When Jean first entered therapy for depression, she reported that she had no friends. Although she was intelligent and attractive, this shy twenty-year-old college student needed to gain confidence in her social skills. To help Jean feel more comfortable in social settings, her therapist had her practice conversation skills by role playing them with her. In therapy Jean learned to initiate conversations, ask questions, make appropriate comments, and end conversations gracefully.

After several weeks, the therapist assigned Jean to go to her older sister's Christmas party. All Jean had to do was approach a person she didn't know and start a conversation. Although she was nervous and scared, Jean found the courage to do the assignment. The conversation lasted less than five minutes, but Jean felt great about overcoming her fear and taking action.

Like Jean, some depressed women need self-management skills and might benefit from training in assertiveness, decision-making, problem-solving, and time management. As they gain self-management skills, they will be able to endure the everyday pressures and experience peace and harmony in life. They will see the "symptoms of depression as problems to master and transcend, not as permanent character traits or personality flaws."[8]

TRANSFORMING NEGATIVE THINKING
INTO REALISTIC THINKING

Cognitive therapy, developed by psychiatrist Aaron T. Beck, M.D., at the University of Pennsylvania, is based on the idea that depression is linked to thinking. How a person feels is a direct product of how she thinks, or as the Bible says, "For as he thinketh in his heart, so is he" (Proverbs 23:7, KJV).

Cognitive therapy pinpoints problem patterns of thinking. The cognitive therapist takes the role of an active guide, training patients to:

◆ Label and understand self-sabotaging distortions such as "overgeneralization" and "poisoning the positive" (see chapter 9)
◆ Recognize when they're using distortions
◆ See why they think the way they do and teach them how to change their thinking

Cognitive therapy rests on the assumption that when thinking changes, feelings change. To accomplish this goal, a therapist may help patients substitute realistic thoughts for negative ones. For example, Cora, a thirty-year-old single woman, consulted a cognitive therapist to help her deal with feelings of depression and loneliness. During treatment, the therapist realized Cora was adding to her problem by labeling her single status a curse. He had her make a list of the benefits of being unmarried, such as independence and control over her time and money. She was to make her list and review and add to it every day for several weeks. Over time, she realized that her singleness had some definite advantages and wasn't the curse she had thought. Deliberately thinking realistically helped lift her depression.

A cognitive therapist might direct the patient to "test out" her thinking. Denise sought help for her depression with a cognitive therapist after trying to fight it on her own for four months. During that time she gradually withdrew from her friends. One of the first things she told the therapist was, "I don't have any friends." He suggested she "test out" her thinking by inviting some of her "former" friends to her house for coffee.

"No, I couldn't do that," Denise responded. "They wouldn't come. No one cares for me."

The therapist persisted, and Denise agreed to give it a try. She called four friends. Three of them agreed to come for coffee. The other one regretted that she couldn't come because of a previous appointment. They all expressed pleasure in hearing from her. They said things like, "I've missed you," "I've been praying for you," and "I was wishing I would hear from you."

In addition, therapists might ask patients to fill out rating forms, write down recurrent negative thoughts, and describe difficult encounters with other people. Sometimes a patient might be asked to write her negative thoughts in one column and rebuttal thoughts in another column. A therapist might encourage patients to wear a wrist counter and click it each time they have a negative thought. Focusing on these assignments often breaks rumination and speeds recovery.

Many depressed women take on excessive, inappropriate responsibility for negative events in their lives and underestimate the power they have to influence those events. Cognitive therapy is geared to helping a woman regain a sense of mastery over her life by learning to master her thoughts. This is often enough to lift depression, particularly when it's combined with behavioral change. Behavioral therapy and cognitive therapy are often used in combination, referred to as cognitive/behavioral therapy.

UNTANGLING PEOPLE PROBLEMS

If a woman conceives of her life as a continuous thread, then depression is a place of snarling, tangling, and stoppage. Since harmonious relationships are critical to her well-being, nothing tangles a woman's life more than people problems. *Interpersonal therapy* (IPT) addresses people problems by helping a woman improve the ways she interacts with others.

The interpersonal therapist looks for a problem in one of four major areas:

1. *Losses (ending of relationships) and related problems such as abnormal grief reactions and unresolved grieving.* IPT helps with the mourning process and assists the client in finding new social relationships.
2. *Conflicts.* IPT helps the client examine disputes she may be involved in with a spouse, a boss, a friend, a relative, or coworker. The client learns communication, negotiation, and assertion skills to resolve the disputes.
3. *Role transitions.* Leaving home, having a baby, divorce, retirement, and some job changes involve difficulties as a woman moves from one way of being to another. IPT evaluates the lost role and encourages expression of loss-related emotions. The therapist also assists and supports the client in developing skills suitable for the new role.
4. *Social deficits.* Some women have difficulty in their relationships because they have never developed strong interpersonal skills or they have difficulty encountering new situations because they feel their resources are not sufficient. IPT helps a woman develop relationship skills and strengthen her inner resources.

The person seeking interpersonal therapy is called a "client" instead of a "patient." She is not regarded as "sick" or in need of a "cure."

After reviewing with the client her current relationships, the therapist assists her in setting goals and developing strategies for meeting those goals. The client may want to communicate more effectively in her current relationships or develop new relationships. In terms of the goals, homework assignments are mutually developed. Therapist and client regularly discuss outcomes and modify strategies until the client achieves her goals.

Unfortunately, IPT it is not available everywhere. If a woman recognizes that her depression is people-related and there's not an IPT therapist near her, she might say to a general therapist, "I always seem to be in conflict with someone. I get one situation straightened out and another one erupts. I want to break this cycle. Would you help me?" Most therapists are familiar with the kinds of skills needed for improving relationships, and most are willing to adapt their techniques to meet the needs of the client.

IN A GROUP SETTING

Group therapy is psychotherapy in a group setting. Instead of a one-on-one session of patient with therapist, several people (usually around six) meet with a therapist. The group is led by a trained therapist and may be interpersonally oriented, behaviorally oriented, or insight oriented. The group provides cohesiveness and support, is a safe place to share feelings and experiences, and gives feedback about interpersonal skills and problem solving.

Since women often feel drained of their energy and isolated from others, a group setting can break the isolation they feel. Interaction with others replenishes energy and gives women the people connection they need and want. A group of all women encourages exploration of the sources of their depressed feelings, especially those sources to which women are more prone. Women share the bond of being influenced by similar cultural expectations. They have the camaraderie of "We are in this together."

As they share feelings and experiences, women realize they are not alone. This can be very reassuring to a depressed woman. It's not uncommon for her to think, "I'm the only one who has ever felt this way." Sharing with other women takes away the loneliness and offers insight and encouragement.

In group therapy, Meredith was able to talk about her depression and gain insight and support from the other women in the group. Meredith and Tom had finally acquiesced to their parents' desire for a grandchild and had a baby. Meredith took a year's maternity leave to care for the baby, but Tom kept right on with his gone-every-night schedule as a high-volume insurance salesman. Although the grandmothers wanted a grandchild, they both lived out of state. Each took a few days off work to help Meredith when she came home from the hospital. After that she was on her own. The baby was colicky, allergic to milk, and had episodes of intense screaming. Meredith started having bouts of crying, too. She wondered over and over why she had ever agreed to have this child. She felt so detached from him. One day after she had been up with the baby four times during the night, he started screaming again late in the morning. Meredith snapped and started shaking him. Then she caught herself. *What's happening to me? Am I going crazy?*

She called her doctor, and he encouraged her to join a therapy group for new mothers sponsored by a local hospital. It was just the right thing. She found other mothers there who had had careers and were now trying to navigate the waters of motherhood. To them she was able to admit, "I never wanted this baby." Confessing that helped her grow to love her baby. Together the group members supported each other through their postpartum depressions and exchanged coping skills.

Group therapy may also be particularly helpful to people whose depression is related to bereavement or chronic illness. Members benefit from the example of others who have successfully dealt with similar problems, and survivors gain self-esteem by serving as role models for newer patients.[9]

The group provides a safe environment where women can risk new behaviors they may not be ready to try in the outside world. Participants can develop and nurture communication skills that are valuable in every facet of life and can formulate effective action strategies together. They can support each other as they carry out their strategies, measure the effectiveness of the strategies, and suggest modifications when needed.

Marital therapy and family therapy are two forms of group therapy. A woman's depression is not always limited to her. It may be symptomatic of a troubled marriage or family, or it may be the result of problems in the marriage or family. She may want to seek marital therapy (the therapist works with husband and wife together) or family therapy (the therapist sees parents and children together).

To get well, a depressed woman needs to know two things: (1) What is making me unhappy? and (2) What can I do about it? Those questions can be answered in behavior therapy, cognitive therapy, interpersonal therapy, and group therapy. The skills a woman gains in therapy—whether it is recognizing her distorted thinking patterns, improving her conversation skills, or scheduling her time—reduces her future risk of depression. Her new skills improve the quality of her life and prepare her for coping with future stressful events.

Chapter Seventeen

Meeting the Difficulties Head-On

⌒

"Why didn't you prepare us?" Janice, a former student in my marriage and family class, said. "After having a baby, my feelings really scared me. When my baby cried and cried with the colic, I cried, too. I sometimes felt I was on the edge of being out of control. Once I even started screaming. Why didn't you tell our class that motherhood could be like this? If you had, I would have been more prepared to deal with it."

I wouldn't want to make the same mistake in presenting the treatment options for depression. The brevity of the last three chapters may give the impression that treatment is simple and routine. It can be simple for some women, just as some new mothers never feel on the edge of being out of control. But for others, seeking treatment involves difficulties. Let's look at the major ones so we can meet them head-on.

RELUCTANCE TO SEEK HELP

Some women see depression as a character flaw. To seek help is, in their eyes, the same as admitting, "I'm a weak person." A Christian woman may reason, "If I were a strong Christian, I wouldn't be depressed. If I really had faith, I wouldn't have to seek anybody's help but God's."

Others may resist getting help because they think they ought to be able to deal with the depression on their own. As one woman said, "I'm arrogant. I thought I was as smart as anyone; no one could tell me anything about my problems that I didn't already know."

No one has all the answers to life's problems. Seeking the help of a mental health professional offers a woman insights and solutions she hasn't thought of and widens her resources. It also gives God more channels in which to work. He can expose wrong or sinful attitudes and correct wrong behavior.

A woman who seeks help can gain victory over the overwhelming stresses in her life. Taking an antidepressant may be part of the help to gain that victory. Seeking professional help is an action that says, "I'm taking responsibility for my life." It puts an end to the victim mentality that says, "I'm doomed to a life of suffering. I can't do anything about my situation."

DIFFICULTY IN FINDING THE RIGHT PROFESSIONAL

The best professionals for treating depression are those who:

1. *Are not exclusively committed to one type of treatment.* Remember, various methods are used to treat depression—none of which is perfect or 100 percent successful.

If a woman seeks the help of a professional committed to one treatment, she limits her options. For example, some psychiatrists are committed to the biological view of depression and see depression as strictly a medical illness to treat with medication. Since medication doesn't work for everyone, it's wiser to see a professional who is open to all options.

2. *Are knowledgeable about antidepressants.* When a woman chooses to take antidepressants, she needs a professional who will closely supervise the treatment. Dosage levels and possible side effects must be carefully and knowledgeably monitored. As stated earlier, general practitioners may know too little about depression, prescribe the wrong drug, offer too little of the correct drug, or not explain side effects.

3. *Have the patient or client's confidence.* An important part of healing takes place as a result of the warmth, support, and validation the patient receives from the professional.

4. *Respect the patient.* A woman shouldn't go back to a professional who does or says anything that smacks of sexual innuendo, doesn't respect her beliefs, or refuses to allow discussion on anything spiritual. The best way to find the right professional is to ask friends and acquaintances. My beautician, a fine Christian woman who has been in busi-

ness for years, once told me, "If there's something wrong with the way a doctor is practicing, I'm going to hear about it from my customers. Anyone can make a mistake, but repeated mistakes add up until a reputation is established."

I also recommend calling the psychiatry department of a nearby medical school or the local chapter of a mental health association. Community mental health centers and the psychiatry department of a general hospital will also be able to help.

UNREALISTIC EXPECTATIONS

Some women may be tempted to get off the road to recovery because it takes too long to see the desired improvements.

Antidepressants do not provide immediate relief. Remember, they have to reach therapeutic dosage levels before they reach their full effectiveness. After four weeks, a woman may be tempted to stop taking her medication, thinking, *I knew it. This isn't going to help.*

It can take at least six weeks for the medication to reach the correct levels. If after that time a woman still doesn't see any improvement, she might ask her doctor to change dosage or change antidepressants. If her doctor isn't willing to work with her on making changes, she needs to change doctors.

Psychotherapy also takes a few weeks before you see improvement. Most experts recommend against "therapist shopping." A woman shouldn't try a therapist for one session and then move on to another and possibly another. It's best to pick a therapist and try to make the relationship work for at least eight weeks. If after that time there is no improvement, she needs to look for another therapist.

Finding another therapist can be discouraging. It's tempting to give up, but finding a good therapist is critical. Competence is important, but so is the chemistry between patient and therapist. It's one of the best predictors of successful treatment.[1]

In therapy, a woman shares her most intimate thoughts and feelings, so it's important to find a therapist who puts her at ease.[2] The therapist may have many brilliant techniques, but if he lacks warmth and concern, she may become annoyed and mistrustful.[3] As unassertive as many depressed patients are, she may not express her negative feelings.

"This will sabotage the therapy."[4] She may make the therapy fail as a way of letting the therapist know how let down and hurt she feels.[5]

DISCOURAGED BY THE COST

For those whose health insurance limits payment for mental illness or who don't have insurance and whose budget has no room for additional expenses, professional treatment can seem prohibitive. Some antidepressants are expensive, and they should be taken for at least six months. Private psychotherapists charge from $50 to $150 or more for one session.

With rising health costs, many insurance companies are singling out mental health and imposing limits on the number of therapy visits. "Insurance plans generally pay for 80 percent of medications, but only half of therapy."[6] According to the American Psychological Association's national task force on women and depression, 37 million Americans, many of whom are working, have no health insurance.[7] Medicaid coverage of individuals with incomes below the poverty level continues to decrease,[8] and a large proportion of Medicaid recipients are women.

A woman in any of these financial situations may conclude, "There's nothing I can do." That's a position she doesn't want to be in. "Many depressed individuals will go through a phase in which they *stubbornly refuse* to do anything to help themselves. The moment this crucial motivational problem has been solved, the depression typically begins to diminish."[9]

Here are some ways a woman with limited means can help herself.

Take advantage of free events. Mental health clinics, some churches, and mental health associations offer free lectures and question-and-answer sessions on depression, which give insight and information as well as provide opportunity for interaction with professionals and others seeking help.

National Depression Screening Day, which is usually in early October, is an event offering free testing to determine whether a person is depressed or likely to become so. The testing is usually followed with a consultation with a mental health professional. Sites are registered in all fifty states and the District of Columbia.

Ask for less expensive drugs and comparison shop. As I interviewed some pharmacists, I showed them a list of all the antidepressants mentioned in chapter 16 and asked, "What would a month's prescription cost for each of these?" A month's prescription (one to three pills a day for thirty days) ranged from $4.79 to $249.09. Some were indeed high, but several were less than $20 a month.

All antidepressants have about the same success rate, so it pays to do some research. Prices for antidepressants vary from druggist to druggist. Generic versions of some of the older antidepressants are also available. Comparison shopping can help cut costs.

Look for agencies that offer free or reduced rates. Local mental health clinics and other nonprofit agencies may offer therapy on a sliding scale based on a woman's income. Free counseling services are available for female students on many large college campuses. Large churches may have trained counselors on their staff; many pastors are trained in counseling. Hospitals and the military have chaplains. Large companies may offer psychological services to their employees.

Not all of these agencies will have highly trained psychotherapists, but they will have people knowledgeable about avenues for getting treatment. If they can't help, they will know where or how a woman might get affordable treatment.

A mildly or moderately depressed woman can join a self-help or support group. These groups are not designed to do therapy, but they can provide support, interaction, and insight. Group members share their experiences with depression, learn coping skills, distribute information about new treatments, and refer people to doctors and therapists in their community. To locate a depression support group, a woman can contact the Mental Health Association in her area or use the local newspaper listings of self-help groups.

Some Bible study and prayer groups can offer similar support. For this type of group to be helpful, the members must be honest strugglers who do not offer cliché answers to life's hurts. A woman's depression would only worsen in a group where members wear polished halos.

RELUCTANCE TO TAKE ANTIDEPRESSANTS

"In one survey, 70 percent of those questioned said they'd use medicine for a headache, but only 12 percent would touch an antidepressant."[10] Some of their reluctance may be due to the rumors they've heard. They "may have been deterred by an anti-Prozac campaign by the Church of Scientology, which asserted that the drug triggered suicide or violence. The Scientologists' claims, however, were refuted by the Food and Drug Administration in 1991."[11]

People who have a true chemical imbalance and have severe depression need antidepressants in order to return their mood to normal. Antidepressants are also helpful to those whose depression affects daily functioning. Antidepressants allow them to work and take care of their responsibilities until the depression lifts.

Likewise, being less moody and having more energy can help a depressed woman work through what might have caused her depression. "Pills don't solve life's problems, but they can put people in a better position to solve the problems themselves."[12]

Antidepressant drugs were the first answer for Berenice, who shares her experience in Julia Thorne's book, *You Are Not Alone.*[13] Berenice spent years being sad and not living up to her potential. Then she got a new job, moved to a new city, and found a new doctor. After diagnosing Berenice with chronic low-grade depression, he prescribed Zoloft. Zoloft made her feel better than she had felt in years. She said, "I finally got some initiative."[14]

She started reading about depression and discovered that it runs in families. As she looked back over her family history, she realized that most members of her family were heavy drinkers, so she joined Al-Anon (the support group for children of alcoholics).

At Al-Anon meetings, she learned how to recognize ways she emotionally protected herself. That made her curious. She thought, "Maybe there's something else I can do besides take a pill."[15] She went to the library where she found books on cognitive therapy. Through the county mental health service, she located a cognitive therapist. After working with the cognitive therapist for four years, she said, "I'm not chronically depressed anymore and I don't take the antidepressant. There's no question that medication gave me the strength to fight my illness."[16]

MAKING MEDICAL TREATMENT A CURE

Because antidepressants restore chemical balance, women might mistakenly think they cure depression. They don't. "The reason a person continues to do well after the antidepressant medication is stopped is that the depression has run its course."[17] Antidepressants may treat the symptoms of depression but they do not cure it. It's similar to insulin and diabetes. The insulin does not cure diabetes, but it allows the diabetic person to live. If a woman sees drugs as a cure, she may not deal with the issues that triggered her depression. She reasons, "I'm not responsible for my moods, it's my body chemistry." That sounds so much more respectable than, "I'm depressed because of the conflict in my marriage," or "I'm depressed because life is not what I thought it would be."

Those who use antidepressants as a quick fix without dealing with underlying problems set themselves up for developing a dependence on drugs. While antidepressants are not addictive in the usual sense, a woman may come to depend on them. She relies on drugs rather than developing new skills and new insights for living.

After one episode of depression, a woman has a 50 percent chance of having another episode. The chances of having a third after two episodes without treatment are even greater. After three episodes, the chances of having a fourth episode jumps to 90 percent.[18] To keep depression from recurring, a woman needs to acquire new skills and new insights. She needs to develop a depression-resistant lifestyle.

PART FOUR

CAN I BECOME MORE RESISTANT TO DEPRESSION?

Chapter Eighteen

Getting the Support You Need

Have you ever noticed how some clothes snag more easily than others? The nature of the fabric, such as a loose weave, makes it easily catch on the corner of a filing cabinet or car door. The little holes or tears that result have to be mended right away. If they aren't, the surrounding threads ravel. The hole or tear will grow in size until the item can't be worn in public.

Once I had a neighbor who was very good at repairing small holes in fabric. She called it darning. She carefully selected thread to match the material. She weaved the thread in and out with tiny stitches until I could scarcely tell where the hole was. Her interlacing stitches rescued garments and strengthened them for further wear.

When a woman becomes depressed, the fabric of her life is snagged. How can she "darn" it to prevent depression from occurring or recurring? What threads can she weave into her life to build resistance to depression? We can spot the right threads by looking back through this book at what we've learned about depression, recovery, and why women are particularly vulnerable. One obvious thread is relationships, especially relationships with other women. When this thread is woven into the fabric of your life, it increases your chances for happiness and optimum mental health.

WOMEN NEED OTHER WOMEN

Men have buddies. They bowl, fish, hunt, and work on old cars together. But when a man has an intimate friend, it's usually his wife.

He tells her his innermost secrets and confidences.

A woman may have a friend in her husband, but she also needs female friends. As one woman lamented, "No matter how much I enjoy my job and love my husband and children, they are not enough." A woman may not be able to share everything she wants to say with her husband (father, brother, male friend). It's not that he's cruel or inconsiderate, it's just that he can't always give her the response she wants. Women want to be "listened to." Being heard is not enough; women want to tap that I-know-how-you-feel response from their listeners, to sense that others are sharing, caring, supporting, or identifying with them in their time of need. Some things a woman wants to talk about will prevent her male listener from responding with that I-know-how-you-feel response.

With our sensitivity to context, we may want to share more than the men in our lives care to hear. We want to share our interest in people and their reactions. Many of us feel tuned out by our husbands or other male listeners when we insist on including too many details. Other women are usually more interested in the details and therefore are more satisfying listeners.

(A married woman's conversations with her friends are not to take the place of conversations with her husband. A woman shouldn't be telling her friends things she should be telling her husband. That would seriously harm the marriage relationship. A married woman needs intimate sharing with her husband *and* with her friends.)

Women nurture each other through friendships. We want and need mothering touches. We want someone to do for us the kind of sensitive, caring things we do for others. A young woman sees the tired look of her friend with three preschoolers and says, "Let me watch the children this afternoon, so you can take a nap." Another sees the tense look of the female secretary at the next desk and says, "Lunch is on me today." Such nurturing returns to women some of the emotional investment they make in others and helps to replenish their emotional strength.

Nurturing one another helps us navigate the various stages of the life cycle by providing support, encouragement, and information along the way. When Clara was pregnant, her friends threw her a shower and talked with her about her baby's development. After the baby was born, they supported her in the early days of motherhood. They brought casseroles and salads to help with meal preparation. One friend cleaned her house. Another took her ironing home. Two friends who nursed their babies encouraged Clara to nurse and supported her with helpful information and advice. Women often continue this camaraderie as they raise their children, checking with each other for advice and support. When the nest empties, they share their feelings and discuss plans for the future. More than likely, they will still be nurturing each other after their children are grown and their husbands have died.

Women need each other so much that we are even teased about it:

Question: How many women does it take to change a light bulb?

Answer: Five! One to turn it, and four to form a support group.

Despite the need we have for relationships with other women, developing and sustaining friendships is not easy to achieve in today's world.

A SOCIETY UNCONDUCIVE TO FRIENDSHIPS

Women are busier than ever before. Our lives are complicated and tightly scheduled. Many of us have so many responsibilities that we don't have time to talk about our feelings or encourage someone else to talk. We worry about how we're going to get our work done or meet our responsibilities. Meeting deadlines and maintaining schedules doesn't allow time for intimate sharing.

For some of us, every moment has to be filled with productive activity. Some women's lives are so intense they don't know they are lonely until a crisis hits. They long for someone to talk to about what happened with them, but there's no one to call.

In today's transient society, a woman makes a close friend and finds she has to move, or her friend has to move. In years past female camaraderie was provided within the family—mother and daughter or sister and sister. Now women are often forced to live away from their extended families.

On top of all that, our culture tells women to be strong and independent. This emphasis makes it hard for some women to admit they need others. In the midst of our busyness, we need the support of other women. We need to be listened to, mothered, and encouraged.

KNOTS IN THE THREAD

When I tried copying my neighbor's darning style, my thread often got knots in it. That meant starting over. Sometimes I would get so discouraged I would decide the garment wasn't worth mending.

The relationship thread can have its own share of knots. Women need to know what some of the knots are so they can untie them and find the friendships they need.

1. *Not being friendly.* We've all heard that "To have a friend, you must be a friend." To gain friends you must be friendly. If a woman has difficulty making friends, she needs to ask herself if she is saying or doing something that makes others think she doesn't want friends.

When a pastor of a church I belonged to resigned, some of us bought a farewell gift for his wife. She graciously accepted our gift, but then she said, "I hope your next pastor's wife won't be as lonely as I have been here." Her comment shocked us. We had no idea she had been lonely. Both she and her husband talked about how busy they were. They complained, "We never have any time to ourselves." We thought we were doing them a favor by not bothering them.

2. *Unwillingness to risk rejection.* Unfortunately, reaching out to make friends contains an element of risk. The other person may not respond positively to our overtures.

Some women may silently send out signals or drop hints in hopes that other people will reach out. The signal that is so clear to one woman may not be noticeable to the person she is trying to attract. A woman can't count on others to read her mind. If she wants a friend, she may have to extend her hand, take the risk, and say, "Hi, I'm. . . . Let's have coffee sometime."

3. *Unwillingness to be flexible.* Most women want friends who share their interests, are good listeners, and can sense what they are feeling. Women are fortunate when they can find such friends, but sometimes women may find themselves in a stage of life or in a location where a friend who possesses these qualities is not available. Refusing to settle

for less can leave a woman lonely and feeling inadequate.

Karen discovered this when she moved. On her block, she was the only woman with young children who stayed home with them. Karen missed the camaraderie she had in her old neighborhood with other mothers with young children. The only other woman home during the day was a gray-haired woman who used a cane. When Karen watched the woman slowly walking to her mailbox, she would sigh wistfully. "If only there were someone home during the day—someone my age— that I could talk with."

One day when loneliness got the best of Karen, she invited the older woman for tea. To Karen's delight, the woman asked her lots of questions about her children. Karen liked the attention and the opportunity to talk. It wasn't quite like old times, but Karen did have an opportunity to talk about what was important to her. She never expected to become friends with someone old enough to be her grandmother.

4. *Unwillingness to reciprocate.* We need to ask ourselves, *Am I willing to do for others what I want them to do for me?* We shouldn't expect to receive what we're not willing to give. Friends need to take turns listening to one another. A good way to lose a friend is by continuing to unload on her.

When a friend is tired, it's not a good time to ask her to listen. Listening requires enormous energy. Asking friends to listen when they are exhausted is like asking them to go on a nine-mile hike the minute they cross the finish line of a marathon race.

5. *Unwillingness to be direct.* Some of us expect our friends to accurately assess our needs. We expect our friends to be mind readers. When they don't guess correctly, we feel disappointed.

To avoid disappointment, we need to be direct. If we need "listening to," then we need to say, "I need to talk. I'm not looking for a solution; I just need to vent my feelings."

On the other hand, when we want our listener's opinion, we should say, "I really value your opinion on this. What do you think?"

A clear request is the best way to get what we need and want in a conversation, but it may be hard to do. Many women who are assertive on behalf of their children or their friends are uncomfortable using those assertion skills on their own behalf.

Obviously, there are knots in the thread of relationships. But if we recognize the knots, and patiently and realistically work at untying them, we can gain valuable support for resisting depression. We'll be able to say with Dee Brestin, author of *The Friendships of Women*, "My friends are an oasis to me, encouraging me to go on. They are essential to my well-being."[1]

Chapter Nineteen

Your Sense of Self

A long time ago, Hannah Whitall Smith made this connection of self with depression.

> The greatest burden we have to carry in life is self. The most difficult thing we have to manage is self. Our own daily living, our frames and feelings, our especial weaknesses and temptations, and our peculiar temperaments—our inward affairs of every kind—these are the things that perplex and worry us more than anything else, and that bring us oftenest into bondage and darkness.[1]

The truth of her words has been verified in this book. Many women struggle with cultural expectations, learned helplessness, unrealistic expectations, unexpressed emotions, low self-esteem, deep disappointments, and losses.

To develop a depression-resistant lifestyle, a woman needs a strong sense of self. This is not narcissistic; it is necessary to ensure that she can meet the challenges of life and relationships without burying herself in the process. Strengthening the self promotes a woman's inner security and self-confidence. It gives her the courage to be authentic.

As Smith indicates, strengthening self is not an easy process, but it can be done with effort focused around six key areas: self-awareness, self-expression, self-image, self-direction, self-management, and self-acceptance.

WHAT AM I FEELING AND THINKING?

How is it that a woman who is sensitive by nature may not be aware of her feelings?

+ She may believe that feelings of anger, irritability, grief, and anxiety are wrong. To acknowledge them would be the same as admitting wrongdoing.
+ She may have been so caught up in pleasing others that she's ignored her own feelings. It just never occurs to her to think about what she's feeling.
+ She may have low self-esteem. Unconsciously, she theorizes that her feelings are not worthy of acknowledgment.

Women who are not self-aware are unable to distinguish one emotion from another. They lump everything they feel under the category of "not feeling good."

I was that way. My struggle with depression opened my eyes to my need to recognize what I was feeling. With practice, I've improved. I've read a lot about emotions so I can identify what I'm feeling. When I can label my emotion, I immediately gain some control over it and can find appropriate ways to deal with it.

In addition to asking, *What am I feeling?* a woman needs to ask herself, *What do I think?*

In some families, groups, workplaces, and churches, women's convictions and opinions are not valued. This mindset may be so subtle that inwardly a woman agrees with it. She fails to form her own convictions and opinions or she may form them but not have the courage to express them. The tragedy is, this robs a woman of integrity. It keeps her from acting and speaking from her innermost being.

How do we develop our convictions? By time spent alone, meditating, pondering, and reflecting. Perhaps it's an early morning quiet time when you ask the Holy Spirit to help you recognize your feelings. Perhaps it's a long soak in the bathtub with the door locked and a "do not disturb" sign posted outside, or a stop at a park or library on the way home from work. It can be time just nestled in a comfortable chair after the rest of the household has gone to bed.

How you take time is not important, developing your awareness is. Awareness of your feelings and thoughts is essential to building a strong self.

LET ME TELL YOU HOW I FEEL

Once we recognize our feelings, convictions, and opinions, we need to learn appropriate ways to express them, especially negative emotions. Our motivation for self-expression shouldn't be to hurt, punish, or put down someone else, especially our husbands. There are legitimate ways to express what we need from them, just as Alicia learned.

Alicia resented that her husband didn't help with the housework and the care of their two toddlers. Each afternoon after they picked up the children from day care and arrived home from work, Tom turned on the TV and settled in the recliner. Alicia started dinner, tried to pick up the household clutter, sorted the laundry, and tended to the children. As she stirred the potatoes, she stirred up her resentment. *Why doesn't he see that I need help? They're his children, too. It's not fair that I have to do so much.* Sometimes she would slam the cupboard doors extra hard or drop something to try to get him to say, "Honey, do you need any help?"

The kind of feelings Alicia experienced will always erupt. Her eruption came over spilled milk. At dinner, one of the children turned over a glass of milk. Alicia jumped up to get a cloth, while Tom kept on eating. That did it! Alicia yelled at Tom, "You never do anything around here." Tom yelled back that he did plenty. The fight was on with the children as spectators. Soon they were crying.

Tom slept on the couch that night, and Alicia went to work the next day with a headache. When she asked Lydia, an older coworker, for some extra-strength aspirin, Lydia said, "Let me take you to lunch today." Over lunch, Alicia told Lydia what had happened. Lydia responded, "I've been married thirty years. Do you mind if I give you a few pointers?" Here's what Lydia told her.

Share your need without being accusatory. "You have a legitimate need, but don't turn your feelings into an accusation. Say things like, 'I need to talk,' or 'I really need your help with this' instead of 'You never do anything.'"

Choose the time wisely. "You were both tired and tense when you exploded. You want to get his help, so choose a time for talking when chances for success are better. Maybe the weekend would be better for you. Do it when the children aren't present so you won't be distracted and interrupted."

Expect feedback. "While you see the situation as totally unfair, your husband is going to have his side of the story. Once you have expressed yourself, you need to listen to his side. Then you may need to express your case again, and perhaps again in a logical, calm manner. Communication is about negotiating and compromise, but remember the important thing is having the opportunity to express yourself."

Make a specific suggestion. "While you want to express your feelings, you also want a change. It helps to have some specific suggestions to offer."

Although Alicia didn't have specific suggestions ready, she did take Lydia's advice about an appropriate time. That weekend, while the children were napping, she asked, "Could we talk? I really need your help with something."

"Sure," Tom said. "What's up?"

"I'm sorry I yelled at you the other night about not helping around the house. I feel like I'm drowning under the weight of all I have to do. I don't understand why you don't do more around the house." She told him all the things she had to do each evening.

Tom responded with, "I thought I was doing a lot," and he listed the things he tried to accomplish on the weekend. He also said how much he needed time to unwind at the end of the day. "Honey, my job is extremely stressful. I deal with so many cantankerous people all day, I just want to go into neutral when I get home."

Alicia saw that he was sincere. Then she thought of a suggestion: "Why don't we set aside the first hour when we get home for you to relax in your favorite chair watching television? After that, maybe you could help by taking over the child care for the evening—bathing them and getting them ready for bed."

"Good," he said. "I'd like that. I need to spend more time with the children. Why don't I also clean up the kitchen after dinner? My time to relax could be before dinner, and yours could be after dinner."

When a woman expresses rather than represses her negative emotions, she is more resistant to depression.

BUILDING YOUR SELF-IMAGE

Depression is an illness of low self-esteem. To build resistance against depression is to raise self-esteem. According to Dr. Joyce Brothers, that means working on your self-image. She writes, "Self-image is the root of self-esteem."[2] A woman's self-image includes her abilities, achievements, job, family, economic status, social status, relationships with others, education, and appearance.

For many women, the most critical factor is physical appearance. To continually strive to be thin and forever young is to set a woman up for repeated failure and chronic low self-esteem. What can a woman do?

1. *Learn not to play by the rules or even play the game.* We can pick a weight and a style we can live and be happy with. This way *we* dictate the standard.

2. *Keep a sense of proportion and not blame what is wrong in her life on her looks.* "In ninety-nine cases out of a hundred, the person who believes her looks are blocking her from the life she wants is wrong."[3]

3. *Concentrate on other attributes.* Women have other strengths, such as courage, warmth, and humor, that are more effective than beauty. "A recent series of studies by psychologist Stephen Franzoi at Marquette University established that women who are traditionally feminine, compliant, and nurturing tend to be unhappy with their bodies and want to change them. But women who pride themselves on their intelligence, courage, and drive, as well as on their empathic and nurturing qualities, are happier with their appearance and score much higher on tests of body-esteem. They do not fall into the cultural trap of judging their looks by the way they believe others judge them."[4]

4. *Act "as if."* If we act as if we are attractive, people will see us that way. In his book *Arthur Ashe on Tennis,* Ashe wrote, "Regardless of how you feel inside, always try to look like a winner. Even if you are behind, a sustained look of control and confidence can give you a mental edge that results in victory."[5]

DETERMINING YOUR OWN GOD-GIVEN DIRECTION

While appearance is a critical matter in self-image, it is not the most damaging. "The most damaging kind of self-image may be the result of underestimating yourself, of not letting yourself be all that you could be."[6] This means we are not letting ourselves be the women God designed us to be. We become passive and accept whatever life brings our way. We live in bondage to what others think and to what others demand. To develop a strong self, we need to determine our own direction. One way to do this is by having personal goals that will propel us forward instead of getting us bogged down by what life throws our way. To develop goals, we need to ask ourselves:

+ What do I want out of life?
+ What do I believe God wants me to accomplish in the next ten years? In the next twenty?
+ By the time I die, what will I want to have achieved?

I recommend writing down the answers and looking at them often. Written goals provide tangible direction.

If you've been submerged in passivity, you may have difficulty answering these questions. You may need to take a few weeks—or months—or go on a personal retreat to think about goals.

MANAGING YOUR LIFE

Once you've defined your goals, you may have to make some hard choices about your lifestyle and how you spend time. You may have to eliminate some of the things you're doing. While that's difficult, in the long run it will strengthen you as a person.

Eliminating sources of stress is not easy. For example, role overload is a depression trigger for many women. Giving up one role—not that I'm advocating it—would be an obvious solution. However, a recent broad study by the Families and Work Institute showed that 53 percent of employed women don't want to give up any of their responsibilities at work or at home. It's not a matter of economics. Forty-eight percent of those women surveyed said they would choose to work, even if they had enough money to live as comfortably as they would like.[7]

Some women don't even want to give up the expectations that go with their roles. Wendy is an overworked human-resource manager, a single mother, and a graduate student working on her MBA. With her multiple roles, she looked for ways to save time and asked another mother to drive her ten-year-old daughter home from after-school care. That freed up some time at the end of Wendy's day. The other mother was happy to do it, yet Wendy suffered a lot of guilt over letting her do it. The way Wendy saw it, good mothers pick up their children after school.

If Wendy could have gotten past her unrealistic expectations about what is a good mother, she could see that she was using a good time management skill—enlisting the help of others. Other time management skills include developing a daily schedule, keeping a calendar of activities, making "to do" lists, reserving time for self, and reducing time-killing activities, such as talking less on the telephone.

Besides time management skills, other self-management skills you may need are decision-making, problem-solving, assertiveness, and home organizing skills. If you don't know where to start, ask yourself, *What is preventing me from keeping my goals?* When you look long and hard, it may be in one of these areas.

You can find helpful books and videos on these subjects at the public library or nearest bookstore. Using these tools will be a worthwhile investment, because self-management is necessary if you want to be strong, reduce your stress, and meet your goals.

ACCEPTING YOUR LIMITATIONS

Wendy, the single mother working on her MBA, needs to accept herself as a person with limitations. If she is going to fulfill her roles, she cannot also fulfill all of her expectations of each role. Learning to accept limitations is critical to preventing chronic stress and overload.

Acceptance is an underrated concept. Acceptance is not equal to passivity. It means recognizing what can be changed and what can't. It means being at peace with what can't be changed and being free to enjoy life. Many people prone to depression are unduly hard on themselves. They are unwilling to forgive themselves and they make unrealistic self-demands. No mistakes allowed. Their unrealistic expectations provide none of the slack they give to others.

I had to learn to accept myself as a sinner. There's always been within me an earnest desire to do right. An A+ would not have been too high a grade for the effort I put into living the Christian life. (This doesn't mean the results were any better or any worse than anybody else's life; it does mean that I tried very hard.) Unconsciously, I felt that if I kept reading the Bible, studying, praying, and being obedient, the day would come when I would do everything right. That day never arrived.

To develop a strong self, I had to accept myself as a sinner—albeit a forgiven sinner. This acceptance helped me learn to live with myself. While I still try hard to live the Christian life, I don't spend days berating myself for the inevitable errors I make. A great deal of energy can be tied up in trying to do everything right—energy that could be given over to the enjoyment of life.

Accepting myself as a sinner also helps me to be myself with others. Admitting my struggle with sin brings me closer to others rather than separates me from them, as I had once feared. It also makes me more conscious of how much I need God's help to live.

Women can strengthen self by accepting who they are—people with limitations who make mistakes. Self-acceptance brings peace and a strength to meet the challenges and demands of life. No one has to live with depression. We won't if we work to build a depression-resistant lifestyle that includes strengthening self.

Chapter Twenty

Transforming Your Negative Thoughts

~

When Betty's husband died, she chose to see a therapist to help her through the grieving process. Although the therapist wasn't a cognitive therapist, she pointed out that Betty had a pessimistic ruminating response style. At Betty's last session, the therapist told Betty she might want to read some books like *Feeling Good: The New Mood Therapy* or *Learned Optimism* to work on changing her response style.

Betty didn't see it as a problem until Christmas time. The hustle and bustle of the season, the parties, and the family get-togethers all reminded Betty how alone she was. She began to think, *Everybody has family but me. Christmas is for families. I have no one to be with. What will I do on Christmas Day? I will be so miserable. I'll probably never get over it.*

After a few days of thinking like that, Betty couldn't stand it. She headed for the library. By reading books on cognitive therapy, she learned about cognitive distortions and pessimistic ruminations. She also learned she was going to have to battle both to keep from being depressed. She could do that by distracting herself, recognizing cognitive distortions, compiling contrary evidence, disputing self-criticisms, and questioning imperatives.

DISTRACT YOUR FOCUS

We learned earlier that a distracting response style produces less depression, especially for those with a ruminating response style. (Obviously the severity or suddenness of some events would call for reflecting and contemplating. If you've lost a loved one, for instance, you need to feel your loss and not distract yourself. Doing so too soon could lead to suppression or denial, which may eventually cause depression.)

If you're ready, here are some distracting actions you can do:

1. *Change locations.* If you're at home, you might go to work or church, the mall, a park. If you are at work, you might leave the building and take a walk.
2. *Tackle a difficult project that will command all of your attention.*
3. *Participate in a sport or activity that would require you to use your mind or that gives you pleasure.* Go to a concert, a play, or a movie.
4. *Visit someone in a nursing home or hospital.* You must focus on the other person, otherwise visiting a nursing home or hospital might add to your pessimistic ruminating.

Distracting activities relieve a depressed mood or substantially reduce it. When the mood has passed or lessened, you can analyze the event that precipitated the mood.

What is the difference between ruminating when the event happens and analyzing it when the mood has passed? Objectivity. Ruminators get caught up in how miserable they feel and their condition takes on exaggerated proportions. This interferes with their attention and concentration, and they begin to feel helpless. When analysis is postponed until the mood has passed or has lessened, their appraisal is much more objective.

When you engage in action to distract yourself, you increase your chances for control and reduce your sense of helplessness.

RECOGNIZE COGNITIVE DISTORTIONS

You may think, *I don't have any self-deprecating inner thoughts,* or *My thinking couldn't be distorted.* Far more people than realize it live in the shadow of pessimism. That's because cognitive distortions run through our minds automatically. They come in and make themselves at home. We become so comfortable with them we don't even know they're there.

As we've already discussed, one route for gaining awareness of automatic thoughts is to seek the help of a cognitive therapist (see chapter 16). If that seems extreme or is not viable, what else can you do to became aware of your automatic thoughts?

When you feel depressed about something, you can try to identify a corresponding negative thought you had just before feeling depressed. Cognitive distortions take on the form of an internal conversation. Self accuses self: *I'm no good, I'm a complete failure.* This internal conversation continues even when you're talking with someone else.

When I seek to identify my negative thoughts, it helps me to have quiet surroundings and the assistance of the Holy Spirit. In a quiet place, I ask the Holy Spirit to reveal what automatic thought messages I'm speaking to myself. Sometimes simply recognizing the thought message is enough to dissolve my bad mood: *So that's it; that was what was making me feel so blue.* At times, recognition is not enough. Other skills are needed to battle automatic thoughts full of distortions.

COMPILE CONTRARY EVIDENCE

When my youngest child was in his last year of high school, I lost some of my enthusiasm for teaching. The students became adversaries; I was certain they didn't respect me any longer.

Because I'm vulnerable to depression, I didn't want my down feelings to escalate. I asked the Holy Spirit to show me the automatic thought behind my feelings. In those prayerful moments, I realized that my negative feelings were connected to Ben leaving home. The automatic thought flitting through my mind was, *My students won't be interested in my opinions any longer once I don't have a child living at home.*

In my mind, having a child at home was a connection with youth. As long as Ben was home, my students would be interested in what I had to say. From this I overgeneralized, *My life is over.*

Sounds irrational, doesn't it? My automatic thoughts *were* irrational; yet they were so convincing to me that just recognizing them did not dissolve them. I had to compile contrary evidence. This is the process I followed.

◆ Fact: Had one student ever checked me out before taking my class? "Mrs. Poinsett, do you have any children living at home? If you do, I want to take your class. If you don't, I will seek another instructor." No, not one student had ever asked if I had children at home.

+ Fact: Weren't there teachers older than I was doing an effective job of teaching? Yes, there were. Students enrolled in their classes.

+ Fact: Had I ever refused to learn from someone who was old? No, older people are full of wisdom, and I have learned much from them.

+ Fact: Wouldn't God be with me in the next stage of my life? Doesn't God always have significant work for a person to do at any age? As the Bible says, "Even to your old age and gray hairs I am he, I am he who will sustain you" (Isaiah 46:4).

The facts prompted me to pray, "Father, help me move ahead into this new stage in my life. Help me believe I will still have significance as a person and as a teacher." Through prayer, my negative thoughts dissipated and my blue feelings lifted. Two years later I wonder how my thinking could ever have been so irrational!

CHALLENGING WRONG THOUGHTS

If a coworker or an acquaintance criticizes us, we defend ourselves by disputing what he or she says, either verbally or mentally. It's possible to learn to dispute some of our automatic thoughts in the same way.

In our automatic thoughts, we make some awful criticisms of ourselves: "No one likes me." "I look terrible." "I'm a born loser." "Things never go right for me." We take these automatic thoughts and treat them as if they are the absolute truth, but they need to be challenged, as often they are not the truth.

Marion learned to dispute her automatic thoughts by a verbal response. For years, Marion was in a difficult marriage. Her husband was a womanizer, a gambler, and an alcoholic. She was deeply committed to the institution of marriage and put off getting a divorce.

When she finally did divorce, she determined to move forward with her life and got a job and joined a support group for newly divorced people. She was adjusting quite well when her ex-husband moved in with a woman whose house Marion had to pass on the way to work. The only way Marion could get to her job was to drive past this woman's house. Within a few days, Marion felt depressed.

When she discussed her depressed feelings with her support group, they helped her trace them to passing the house where her ex-husband now lived. Knowing her ex-husband was in the house with someone else triggered Marion's negative thoughts. *If I had been a really good Christian, if I had been stronger in my faith, I could have made my marriage work. I'm a failure.*

Marion's group suggested she launch a verbal attack against her automatic thoughts. Seeing the house was her cue to say out loud, "While my marriage did not work out, I am a competent woman. I have raised three children; they have all turned out well. I am respected at my job. I have many friends who care for me. I have parents who love me. I am not a failure."

After several days of verbal disputing on the way to work, Marion reported no longer experiencing any depressed feelings. After a couple of weeks, she could drive by the house without even noticing it.

Joan found that disputing her automatic thoughts by writing worked better for her than a verbal response. Maybe it was because she's an elementary school teacher who keeps her planning book filled with details. When Joan read in the newspaper that the state legislature was trying to pass a law to have all teachers pass a competency test, her heart skipped a beat. She thought, *I always do lousy on tests. They make me so nervous. They will probably ask detailed questions on learning theory, something I haven't thought about since college. I know I will fail and end up losing my teaching job. Then I will have to start all over in another field.*

By bedtime, Joan's anxiety level was so high she couldn't sleep. She turned on the night light, picked up her note pad, and worked at defeating her thoughts through disputing. She noted the automatic thoughts (the cognitive distortions) in one column, and then disputed them with a rational rebuttal in a second column. (Refer to the chart on page 160.)

If you have trouble finding a rational rebuttal, you might consider asking someone else to take a look at your thoughts. Once you have written them down, ask a close friend how she would dispute the thoughts.

AUTOMATIC THOUGHTS	RATIONAL REBUTTAL
I always do lousy on tests.	I sometimes do lousy on tests.
Tests make me nervous.	It's all right to be nervous; most people get nervous. My students get nervous, and they pass their tests.
They will probably ask details on learning theory.	I don't know what kind of test will be given; it may have to do with basic skills—something I'm familiar with. If the test deals with learning theory, they will tell teachers ahead of time. I can do some brush-up work.

QUESTIONING THE VALIDITY OF IMPERATIVES

We all have imperatives inside us, telling us what to do. "Be good," "Be thin," "Work hard," "Smile," "You should tell the truth," "Stop at stop signs," "Put others first." Some of these imperatives come from cultural expectations, some from direct parental instruction, and some come from God. The problem is, the voices may all sound like they come from God, taking on the urgency of God-initiated commands. How can we sort them out?

Ask yourself:

1. *Is this imperative a law?* Is this imperative something such as, "Always drive the speed limit," "Don't run a red light," or "Stop when all school buses stop"? If violating the imperative would result in breaking the law, then it would be wise to obey the imperative. (I realize some people would see some leeway here.) If the imperative isn't a law, then there's some flexibility. Maybe the imperative doesn't have to be obeyed all the time.

2. *Is this imperative a biblical command?* The imperative may be a direct command: "Thou shalt not commit adultery," or "Thou shalt not steal." If it is, then a Christian should obey it.

If the imperative is a biblical principle, perhaps you need to infuse some balance in the way you obey it. For example, while "putting others first" is a biblical principle, it is not a command. Women in care-taking roles who are close to exhaustion must exercise discernment in following this principle to avoid chronic stress. Jesus' life is an example of balance. He put others first, but there were also times when He put Himself first. His ministry was invested in helping others, but He deliberately took time out from needy people to be alone.

3. *If the imperative is not a law nor a direct biblical command, is it realistic?* If not, substitute a more realistic imperative.

In high school, one of my favorite teachers taught me this saying, "There is but one failure and that is not to be true to the very best one knows." That led me to develop an imperative in my life: "Do your best in everything you attempt."

That imperative, coupled with my desire to please God, described my effort in life, always trying to do everything the best way I knew how. Yet the older I got, the more difficult it became to do my best in all my roles—wife, mother, speaker, writer, teacher, gardener, church member, housekeeper, friend, daughter, etc. I knew a lot about how to do each role, but I could not live up to my knowledge. Yet the imperative inside kept saying, *Do your best.*

I had to change that imperative into *Do your best in some areas, accept that you'll do average in others, and even below average in some.* There's still plenty of enjoyment in life in being an average teacher and a below average gardener. When my friends see the small tomatoes in my garden, I smile and say, "I garden for therapy, not for produce."

Becoming aware of automatic thoughts, compiling contrary evidence, disputing negative thoughts, distracting self, and questioning imperatives are five ways we can take control of our thinking. When we do, we will become more optimistic and feel better about ourselves. We will also take a major step toward developing a depression-resistant lifestyle.

Chapter Twenty-One

Building Spiritual Resistance

꙰

When Mary Anne's husband committed her to the hospital's psychiatric ward, the lethargic nature of her depression accompanied her. She wasn't interested in cooperating with the psychiatrist, and she didn't care whether she took her medicine. She didn't care about anything.

Mary Anne felt cold, though, so she asked her husband to bring her a winter robe. In the pocket of the robe was a Scripture printed on a small card: "But may the God of all grace, who called you to His eternal glory through Christ Jesus, after you have suffered a while, perfect, establish, strengthen, and settle you" (1 Peter 5:10, NKJV).

That night, for the first time since she became ill, she felt like praying. "Dear Lord, I never even knew 1 Peter 5:10 was in the Bible. But I'm claiming it for my verse. Whatever You want to do Lord, however long it takes, I'm hanging on to *my* verse."[1]

When it was time for her medicine, she "took" 1 Peter 5:10 along with her medicine by reading it aloud. When she walked the hall, she kept her hand around the small piece of cardboard in her pocket. When she went into the dining room, she repeated the verse before she ate.

A week later, Mary Anne's psychiatrist suggested that she was well enough for her husband to take her away for a while. The trip would give her a chance to adjust gradually before returning home. They headed for the mountains. Wanting to get a particular photograph, her husband went on up the trail. She sat on a bench in the midst of scrubby needled, evergreen piñons. She noticed that every one of them had suffered a porcupine injury, but each of them gave off an intoxicating fragrance. Sitting there quietly, breathing in the clean piñon-scented air, she suddenly realized it was the Lord who had brought her to that place. "Depression, like the porcupine, had made an indelible scar on my life, but the healing sap of God's love that had been promised to me in that one verse of Scripture was flowing."[2]

When her husband came back, Mary Anne ran to meet him.

"Mary Anne," he cried, "your face is shining. You are actually smiling! What has happened to you?"[3]

She said, "The long winter is over."[4]

The spiritual was awakened in Mary Anne through a Bible verse and God's creation. The spiritual assisted in her recovery. The hospitalization was important, the medicine was important, and the spiritual was important. They were all intertwined in her recovery.

We can't compartmentalize our lives. What happens in one area influences the others. What happens in our spiritual lives affects the other areas of our life. We can't discuss building resistance to depression without including the need for spiritual strength.

Spiritual resistance is another thread needed to strengthen the fabric of a woman's life. In this chapter, we are going to look at four ways to do this: observing the Sabbath principle, maintaining a devotional life, promptly dealing with spiritual problem areas, and finding a purpose for living.

"REMEMBER THE SABBATH . . ."

The Sabbath principle goes back to the Ten Commandments: "Remember the Sabbath day by keeping it holy" (Exodus 20:8), and "Six days do your work, but on the seventh day do not work" (23:12). God had the best interests of men and women at heart when He gave this commandment. He knew our lives would need balance for optimum mental, spiritual, and physical health. Rest and worship on a regular basis restore the mind, spirit, and body. When frenetic activity, consumerism, competition, and intense living are put aside, the mind, body, and spirit can unwind and recover, preventing the ravages of chronic stress and overload.

I wouldn't survive long without observing the Sabbath principle. My work week is intense, but on Sunday I refuse to do anything related to teaching and writing. The day begins with worship in which my focus shifts from self to God. A leisurely lunch with family members follows. Then I slowly read the Sunday paper—savoring the activity because it is something I don't have to do. I follow that with a long nap—a real luxury. Sometimes after a particularly stressful week, I wake on Sunday morning saying, "Thank God, it's Sunday."

I'm not suggesting women return to the legalistic observance of the Sabbath prevalent in Jesus' day. I'm not trying to tell Christian women how to observe the Sabbath principle or even when. For Jews, the Sabbath is sundown Friday to sundown Saturday. For the majority of Christians the Sabbath is Sunday, while some Christians rest and worship on Saturday.

What I am recommending is that women regularly and diligently incorporate a break in their lives for worship and rest. When they do they will experience refreshment and renewal. "If you call the Sabbath a delight . . . and if you honor it by not going your own way . . . then you will find your joy in the LORD, and I will cause you to ride on the heights of the land" (Isaiah 58:13-14).

FEEDING YOUR SPIRIT

Practicing the discipline of a daily time of devotional reading and prayer will not prevent depression, but it can build resistance. Here are its benefits.

1. *Devotional reading feeds a woman's spirit.* We need spiritual nourishment to handle the challenges of life and its stresses and disappointments. "Woman does not live by bread alone, but she also needs God's words" (Matthew 4:4, author's paraphrase).

2. *Regular praying keeps a woman on speaking terms with God.* We must get comfortable expressing ourselves to God. This is important because many of the losses we experience cause us to feel alienated from God. At the very time we need His help, we don't feel we can ask Him. A habit of prayer may enable us to seek God's help even when we don't feel like it.

3. *Time alone with God provides time for meditation, pondering, and reflection.* In the aloneness of the moments, when we bring ourselves to God, He responds to us. He can show us things about ourselves, reveal faulty thinking, help us set goals, comfort and guide us. His help becomes

available to us when we open ourselves to Him.

Basically, a woman's devotional time offers God a channel to respond. The channel can get clogged with things like unconfessed sin, unresolved guilt, and unforgiveness. If we readily confess and receive God's help and/or forgiveness, the channel will remain open. If we don't, the channel becomes clogged and depression clouds can begin hovering.

KEEPING THE CHANNEL CLEAR

While depression is not a sin, unconfessed sin can lead to depression. Eventually, unconfessed sin will rear its ugly head. When it does, it may appear as depression. By that time, we may have engaged in cover-up for so long that we see no connection between our sin and our depression.

Guilt accompanies unconfessed sin and can grow out of proportion to the act, affecting our view of life and sapping our energy. The longer we put off dealing with sin and guilt, the tougher they may be to deal with. The wise approach, the way to build resistance to depression, is to confess readily and accept God's forgiveness.

You may want to think long and hard about your life. Is there unconfessed sin? Unresolved guilt? You don't have to wait for depression to strike to remind you to do something about these things. You can confess and seek God's forgiveness now to build resistance to future episodes of depression.

As you seek God's forgiveness, you might also consider forgiving those who have wronged you. I hesitate to advise women to forgive because many of them have experienced some terrible things. To suggest they forgive those who hurt or abused them sounds like asking too much, and yet, forgiveness brings freedom.

Women who were hurt in childhood by people they loved and trusted may find forgiving them particularly difficult. When you forgive, though, you no longer go through life emotionally handcuffed to the person who hurt you. You have better things to do than perpetuate your victimization.

Forgiveness is so difficult that few people can do it on their own. They need God's help. I recommend that women who struggle with wanting to forgive ask for God's help. They may want to exercise prayer therapy as outlined in chapter 13 and also get the assistance of a trusted friend, pastor, or counselor.

While terrible hurts can take only minutes to inflict, forgiving them often requires time. Forgiveness is seldom a simple process. If you need to forgive, you might want to read some books about forgiveness. Two books I've found helpful are *Caring Enough to Forgive* by David Augsburger and *The Key to a Loving Heart* by Karen Burton Mains. An article on forgiveness in *McCall's* magazine[5] mentioned these books: *How to Forgive When You Don't Know How* by Jacqui Bishop and Mary Grunte; *Forgiveness: How to Make Peace With Your Past and Get On With Your Life* by psychologist Sidney Simon and his wife, Suzanne; and *Forgiveness: A Gift You Give Yourself* by Maureen Burns, an incest survivor.

When the forgiveness process is complete, you will have reduced the possibility of being depressed later in life. And you will experience inner freedom that will make your present life much brighter.

A PURPOSE FOR LIVING

Dr. Bernie Siegel, the surgeon who identified the importance of spiritual and emotional concerns as well as the physical to healing, writes that a sense of purpose can do wonders for your health.[6] He quotes a story told by Elizabeth Kubler-Ross about a critically ill woman who was in the hospital. She begged the doctors to help her survive long enough to attend her son's wedding.

> If she could just get to the wedding, she said, it would be all right to die right after that. So they infused her and transfused her to build her up. The day of the wedding all her intravenous lines and tubes were removed. She was dressed up and made up until she looked beautiful, and off she went to the wedding. When she returned to the hospital, everyone was expecting her to stagger onto the ward, lie down and die. Instead, she came back on the ward and said, "Don't forget, I have another son."[7]

While I agree that a sense of purpose can do wonders for a person's health, I don't know if needing a sense of purpose is universal. Some people live life accepting it as it is and moving through its various stages without ever looking for purpose and meaning. They are not analytical or perplexed about what they see. They take life as it comes.

For others, life is not that simple. We want to know why we feel the way we do and why we are here.

Siegel writes that a sense of purpose can be political or personal.[8] For me the purpose has to be eternal. Living for something in this life is not enough. I need a purpose that makes sense out of the nonsense, that makes the humdrum and tedious palatable, that gets me beyond the disappointments of life. I need something that gives significance to what I do. When I lost my purpose, I became depressed. Without that purpose, I could not function.

When one of my sons was struggling spiritually while in his teens, he asked, "Mother, how do you know God is real?"

"I could give you biblical arguments to try to convince you of God's realness," I said. "I could quote you arguments of great theologians, but that's not how I know He is real. I have tried living life with God and without Him. I've learned I can't live without Him."

My struggle with depression showed me that I cannot live without God. Acknowledging His realness and serving Him give me a purpose for living. Aligning myself with His will makes even the insignificant details of life significant. Does that mean His purpose is always evident? No, I operate in the trust that a purpose is being worked out. One of my frequent prayers is borrowed from Jeremiah, who also suffered from depression. "O great and powerful God, whose name is the Lord Almighty, great are your purposes and mighty are your deeds" (Jeremiah 32:18-19). To which I add, "And I know You, God, are working out a purpose in my life."

While I wouldn't want to go through my struggle with depression again, I'm not sorry I experienced it. It solidified my faith. I can say to my sons and to my students, "I know God is real because I've tried living life with Him and without Him. I'll take 'with Him' any day."

I also learned a lot about myself, the illness of depression, and the nature of women. The Bible says, "The LORD blessed the latter days of Job more than his beginning . . ." (Job 42:12, NKJV), and likewise He blessed Brenda Poinsett's life. I would hate to think what my life would have been like if I had not learned what I did about depression. The knowledge changed my life, which is why I share it with you. When we know why we feel the way we do, we can help ourselves and each other.

Chapter Twenty-Two

Ten Ways to Help Her Win

━━━━

Perhaps you're not depressed but you know a woman who is. As her friend, neighbor, Sunday school teacher, Bible study leader, parent, spouse, or sibling, you are in a good position to help. You can initiate contact and offer support and encouragement.

She needs you to reach out to her. Remember, she is groping in darkness—a darkness so thick that it even blocks the light of God from getting through. She needs someone who has access to that light to walk through the darkness with her. You can be God's light to the woman in darkness. Here's how you can help:

1. Spend time with her. "It's important not to assent to his or her wish to withdraw. Telephone frequently and don't be satisfied with leaving a message on the answering machine. The idea is to get the person to engage with you, not just to let him or her know that you're concerned."[1]

2. Encourage her to talk. One pastoral counselor says, "Hope is born when someone really hears us." A depressed woman needs a listening ear. You do not need to probe or offer advice—just let her talk about her feelings.

Keep these guidelines in mind as you listen:

+ *Do not interrupt her* to talk about your own experiences. A lengthy interruption, even if it is well intended, may discourage her. This doesn't mean you should say nothing. You may wish to ask a question now and then for

clarification or make a comment to validate your understanding of what she is saying. But if you intrude with your
experiences in the middle of her story, she will think you're
putting her down or you aren't taking her troubles seriously.

+ *Do not condemn.* No matter what triggered a woman's
depression, she is going to experience guilt. "I shouldn't feel
this way," or "I should be above this sort of thing." Don't
imply that if she were a capable person or a mature
Christian, she would not be depressed.

+ *Don't express shock.* If you've repeatedly tried to get her to say
what's bothering her and then you react in disbelief, she'll
look upon your shock as condemnation. She'll clam up, and
it will be difficult for anyone to get her to talk again. Even
the half-concealed indrawn breath when a depressed person
says a rather startling thing may end the confidence.

Remember this counsel: "Everyone should be quick to listen, slow
to speak and slow to become angry" (James 1:19).

3. Try to understand how she feels. Later on, perhaps, there may
be a right moment to help her seek solutions; but when a woman is
depressed, she just wants you to listen.

Don't say "I know just how you feel" unless you've been depressed.
Instead you might say, "I know depression is an illness that makes people
feel terrible. I'm so sorry this is happening to you. Tell me how you feel."

This may be more difficult than it appears. The complaints of a
depressed person seem exaggerated to the nondepressed; it's hard not to
dismiss them. Parents may be tempted to respond to adolescent depression with denial: "What do you have to be depressed about? These are
the best years of your life!" A husband may say to his depressed wife,
"It's all in your head," or "I know plenty of women who would trade
places with you." A Christian may tell a depressed Christian, "Just praise
the Lord, and you'll get over this." These statements say to the depressed
woman that she is not being taken seriously. The underlying message is,
"I don't understand how you feel, and I do not care to try."

Healing the depression is a process. A woman who is hurting needs
to have her feelings validated as part of the process. Don't try to bypass
the process by giving trite responses to her pain.

4. Don't be overly cheerful. "Like one who takes away a garment on a cold day . . . is one who sings songs to a heavy heart" (Proverbs 25:20). *Today's English Version* of the Bible puts it this way, "Singing to a person who is depressed is like taking off a person's clothes on a cold day or like rubbing salt in a wound."

A depressed person finds a loud, cheerful person irritating. Loud laughter and excessive hilarity grates on her nerves. Don't slap her on the back and say, "Praise the Lord!" or "Cheer up, things could be worse." The depressed woman needs a loving, understanding friend, not a cheerleader.

5. Express your affection openly. Don't criticize her when her self-esteem is at an all-time low. This is the time for kind words, compliments, support, and encouragement. The illness is preventing her from feeling good about herself. Don't say, "How could you feel so low when you've accomplished so much?" or "How could you be depressed when you have such a lovely family?" The point is, she does feel low. What she needs from you is a reminder that her mood is separate from who she is.

Refrain from criticizing or voicing disapproval. . . . You may be tempted, particularly if it's a spouse or child who's ill. Messy disorder and even personal slovenliness are hallmarks of this illness. Curtail any desire you may have to say, "Darling, your hair is filthy." Or, "Can't you do something about that room?" You may, however, say, "Let's go to the hairdresser together," or, "How would you like it if I gave you a massage and a shampoo?" or, "I know you haven't had the energy to clean. I'd like to clean for you."[2]

6. Don't offer simplistic advice. Don't be guilty of offering cheap, unrealistic reassurance that ignores the depressed woman's pain or the seriousness of her situation. This is particularly difficult for Christians who feel we must always be giving witness to our faith. If we can't offer solutions to people's problems, we feel like failures. We feel we must always state the truth and defend God. Job's friends were like that—so intent on defending God that they could not identify with Job. Job said to them, "You, however, smear me with lies; you are worthless physicians, all of you! If only you would be altogether silent! For you, that would be wisdom" (Job 13:4-5).

Every depressed person needs reassurance that no matter what happens she is still a worthwhile person.

7. Lighten her load. The depressed person sometimes feels as if she's drowning in responsibilities. Everyone, she feels, is making exorbitant demands on her. If you can help with just one of those responsibilities, it can give her a burst of energy. Or try to arrange for her to take a break from her responsibilities—a change of scene can break up the clutter of depressive thoughts.

8. Encourage her to get help. She needs professional help if she's having suicidal thoughts; losing a serious amount of weight; experiencing severe physical discomfort in which her health is affected; if the depression is hurting her marriage, her family, or her job; if the depression lasts longer than one year; if it continually recurs.

You will help your friend or loved one tremendously if you investigate the kinds of help available in your area. Find out the particulars and the cost. Share what you find with the depressed woman. Offer to make the appointment for her and go with her. You may need to be firm: "You are depressed. You need help. I know someone who can help. I will go with you."

Be kind but firm in your conviction that the illness can be treated. "Communicating your conviction that help is available and that the person will feel better is extremely important. The self-doubt that is symptomatic of depression spills over into pessimism about things ever being any different. You have to push through that pessimism."[3]

If she continually resists the idea of getting treatment, you may need to speak to her doctor or to a mental health professional. Tell him or her what you have observed. Perhaps the two of you, plus another family member or friend, can decide on a way to coax the depressed woman into treatment.

9. Treat any threat of suicide seriously. A depressed woman may indicate she's thinking of suicide by saying something like this: "My husband will be sorry when I'm gone," "I just can't go on feeling like this much longer," "There's nothing left to live for." Or she may start putting business matters in order. Don't shrug off these signs. Instead, ask about her intentions.

Don't be afraid to come right out and ask, "Do you feel bad enough to kill yourself?" or "Are you planning to kill yourself?" or "Are you so upset that you're thinking of suicide?" This kind of questioning will not plant the idea of suicide in the depressed person's mind. The idea is already there. Questioning will relieve her, giving her a chance to talk. If she is inwardly debating suicide, she may be relieved to express her thoughts.

If she has a well-thought-out plan—naming time, place, and method—she needs immediate help. Get her to a suicide prevention center, a local mental health center, or a doctor at once.

10. *Watch your own reaction.* Remember that depression is an illness that diminishes a person's ability to respond.

> Often, depressed people are. . . unpleasant to be around over long periods of time because they provide little in the way of interactive rewards for those around them. For example, depressed women maintain less eye contact than nondepressed women. They speak less, more softly, and monotonously, and take longer to respond. Their behavior is self-focused and negative, and they communicate a helplessness that suggests the other person just is not doing enough.[4]

This kind of behavior can be frustrating to the person offering help, but don't give up. Be mad at the disease and not the person.

With these ten guidelines, you can be God's light to help the depressed woman walk out of darkness. Don't be concerned about trying to do all of these guidelines perfectly. Your availability and empathy are what matter. These qualities will shine through whatever mistakes you make. Your confidence in her as a person worth salvaging is what's going to help her the most.

Epilogue

Hagar was a woman with limited choices.[1] She was punished by Sarai, the woman she served, and ignored by Abram, the man whose child she was forced to carry. Running away in protest, Hagar fled to the wilderness. The angel of the Lord met Hagar there. He said, "Hagar, where have you come from and where are you going?" That's a good question for us as we end this book.

WHERE HAVE WE BEEN?

As I summarized extensive research on depression, I began by defining it. Depression is an illness. Even though it has different faces and different triggers, it's identifiable. Its symptoms provide us clues to recognize when we or those near us are depressed.

We then explored why women are more predisposed to depression than men. Our bodies, our relationships, the expectations beamed toward us, our response styles when trouble strikes, and deep hurts from the past appear to increase our vulnerability.

The good news, we learned, is that even though we may be more predisposed to depression, we may not get depressed. Even if we do, the treatment menu offers many options. There's something for everyone, from self-help to medication and therapy.

Neither do we have to experience a second or third episode. We can build resistance to depression through gaining support from others, developing a strong self, transforming our thinking, and nurturing our spiritual core.

WHERE'S YOUR KNOWLEDGE TAKING YOU?

With the knowledge we've gained, we can make a difference. We can help ourselves and help others.

In a 1988 survey study of sixty-five women and eighty-three men, ". . . men tended to agree more than women with statements such as, 'Depression is just like any other problem that comes up—you just have to find ways to solve it.' By contrast, women agreed more strongly than men with statements that depression often has biological causes and that it comes on uncontrollably."[2]

My hope is that women who have read this book will see themselves as having control. Unlike Hagar, our options are not limited. We have choices.

The more we understand about why we are at risk, the more we can exercise control. We aren't helpless; we can do something about our situation. With effort, some of us will be able to avoid depression altogether. Others of us won't but we don't have to continue to suffer. We can seek professional help and God's help.

God's angel sent Hagar back to her situation. We might have expected or even wished he would have allowed her to escape, but God had a work for her to do where she was.

God may want us to use our newly gained knowledge about depression where we are. We can offer help to women around us on an individual basis or an organized level. In our churches and organizations, we can share what we've learned and develop support groups so that women who are depressed do not suffer alone. Our sensitivity and compassion can offer hope to those who feel hopeless.

Wherever we are, we can make a difference.

Bibliography

Austin, Elizabeth. "The Secret to Midlife Health." *McCall's*, May 1994, pp. 56, 58, 64, 65, 158.

Barshinger, Clark E., Lojan E. LaRowe, and Andrés Tapia. "The Gospel According to Prozac." *Christianity Today*, 14 August 1995, pp. 34-37.

Beck, Aaron. "Love is Never Enough." *Reader's Digest*, April 1989, pp. 57-58, 61-62.

Begley, Sharon. "Gray Matters." *Newsweek*, 27 March 1995, pp. 48-54.

Bloomfield, M.D., Harold H., and Peter McWilliams. *How to Heal Depression*. Los Angeles: Prelude Press, 1994.

Bowe, Claudia. "Women and Depression: Are We Being Overdosed?" *Redbook*, March 1992, pp. 42, 44, 47 and 78.

Brink, Susan. "Singing the Prozac Blues." *U.S. News & World Report*, 8 November 1993, pp. 76-79.

Brothers, Dr. Joyce. "Men and Women — The Differences." *Woman's Day*, 9 February 1982, pp. 58, 60, 138, 140, and 142.

Brothers, Dr. Joyce. *Positive Plus*. New York: Putnam, 1994.

Burns, M.D., David D. *The Feeling Good Handbook*. New York: A Plume Book published by the Penguin Group, 1989.

Burns, M.D., David D. *Feeling Good: The New Mood Therapy*. New York: The New American Library, 1980.

Colvard, David F., and William P. Wilson. *Christian Counseling Today*, Fall 1995, pp. 14-18.

Copeland, M. S., and Mary Ellen. *Living Without Depression and Manic*

Depression. Oakland, Calif.: New Harbinger Publications, 1994.

Depression Is a Treatable Illness. Rockville, Md.: U.S. Department of Health and Human Services, 1993.

Depression: What Every Woman Should Know. National Institute of Health, Publication No. 95-3871.

"Does Therapy Help?" *Consumer Reports,* November 1995, pp. 734-736, 738-739.

Dowling, Colette. *You Mean I Don't Have to Feel This Way?* New York: Scribner, 1991.

Dranov, Paula. "Tired? Depressed?" *Reader's Digest,* January 1995, pp. 17-20.

Fain, Jean. "Depression Update." *Ladies' Home Journal,* January 1991, pp. 56, 58, and 60.

Fisher, Ph.D., Seymour, and Roger P. Greenberg, Ph.D. "Prescriptions for Happiness?" *Psychology Today,* September/October 1995, pp. 32-37.

Formanek, Ruth, and Anita Gurian, ed. *Women and Depression: A Lifespan Perspective.* New York: Springer, 1987.

Gelman, David; Mary Hager; Shawn Doherty; Mariana Gosnell; George Raine; and Daniel Shapiro. "Depression." *Newsweek,* 4 May 1987, pp. 48-52, 54, and 57.

Goode, Erica E. "For a Little Peace of Mind." *U.S. News & World Report,* 28 September 1987, pp. 98-99, 101-102.

Goode, Erica E., with Nancy Linnon and Sarah Burke. "Beating Depression." *U.S. News & World Report,* 5 March 1990, pp. 48-51, 53, and 55.

Greist, M.D., John H., and James W. Jefferson, M.D. *Depression and Its Treatment.* Washington, D.C., American Psychiatric Press, 1992.

Hancock, LynNell; Debra Rosenberg; Karen Springen; Patricia King; Patrick Rogers; Martha Brant; Claudia Kalb; and T. Trent Gegax. "Breaking Point." *Newsweek,* 6 March 1995, pp. 56, 58-61.

Hart, Archibald D. *Coping with Depression in the Ministry and Other Helping Professions.* Waco, Tex.: Word, 1984.

Hickey, Mary C. "The Exhausted Woman." *Ladies' Home Journal,* March 1994, pp. 86, 90, 92-93.

Hoffman, M.D., Eileen. *Our Health, Our Lives.* New York: Simon & Schuster, 1995.

Hogarty, Donna Brown. "Why Am I So Moody?" *Ladies' Home Journal,*

August 1993, pp. 52, 54-55.

Kane, Ray. "Confessions of a Christian Counselor." *Christian Counseling Today*, Fall 1995, pp. 38-40.

Kiester, Jr., Edwin, and Sally Valente Kiester. "Depression: What You Should Know." *Reader's Digest*, November 1995, pp. 181-82, 184-186, and 188.

Klein, M.D., Donald F., and Paul H. Wender, M.D. *Understanding Depression, A Complete Guide to Its Diagnosis and Treatment.* New York: Oxford University Press, 1993.

Korte, Diana. *Every Woman's Body.* New York: Ballantine Books, 1994.

Lang, Susan S. "Low-Grade Depression." *Good Housekeeping*, January 1994, pp. 72, 74-75.

Laurence, Leslie. "What Women Must Know *Before* Menopause." *Reader's Digest*, October 1994, pp. 109-112. (Condensed from *Ladies' Home Journal*, April 1994, Copyright 1994 by Meredith Corporation, 100 Park Ave, New York, NY 10017.)

Laurence, Leslie. "The Baby-Boomer Health Guide." *Ladies' Home Journal*, April 1994, pp. 73-74, 76, and 78.

Mann, Judy. *The Difference.* New York: Warner Books, 1994.

Margolis, M.D., Ph.D., Simeon, and Peter V. Rabins, M.D., M.P.H. *The Johns Hopkins White Papers on Depression and Anxiety.* Baltimore, Md.: The Johns Hopkins Medical Institutions, 1995.

Mauro, James. "And Prozac For All . . . " *Psychology Today*, July/August 1994, pp. 44, 46-48.

McGrath, Ph.D., Ellen. *When Feeling Bad Is Good.* New York: Henry Holt and Company, 1992.

McGrath, Ellen; Gwendolyn Puryear Keita; Bonnie R. Strickland; and Nancy Felipe Russo. *Women and Depression.* Washington, D.C.: American Psychological Association, 1990.

McKay, David J. "Uncovering Emotion." *Christian Counseling Today*, Fall 1995, pp. 25-27.

Miller, Michael W. "A Little Lithium May Be Just What the Doctor Ordered." *Wall Street Journal*, 23 September 1994, pp. A1 and A4.

Miller, Michael W. "A New Antidepressant Will Challenge Prozac." *Wall Street Journal*, 29 December 1993, pp. B1 and B6.

Nolen-Hoeksema, Susan. *Sex Differences in Depression.* Stanford, Calif.: Stanford University Press, 1990.

Norden, M.D., Michael J. *Beyond Prozac*. New York: Harper Collins, 1995.

O'Reilly, Brian. "Depressed? Here's Help." *Reader's Digest*, April 1994, pp. 151-152, 154, and 157.

Ortberg, John. "Until He Wipes Away the Tears." *Christian Counseling Today*, Fall 1995, pp. 28-31.

Parker, Dr. William R., and Elaine St. Johns. *Prayer Can Change Your Life*. New York: Simon & Schuster, 1957.

Parks, Psy.D, Evan D. "Planning Aftercare for Recurrent Major Depression." *Christian Counseling Today*, Fall 1995, pp. 60-61.

Pekkanen, John. "Keys to a Longer, Healthier Life." *Reader's Digest*, March 1983, pp. 25-28, 30, and 32.

Poinsett, Brenda. *I'm Glad I'm a Woman*. Wheaton, Ill.: Tyndale, 1988.

Poinsett, Brenda. *Understanding a Woman's Depression*. Wheaton, Ill.: Tyndale, 1984.

Salmans, Sandra. *Depression*. Allentown, Penn.: People's Medical Society, 1995.

Scarf, Maggie. *Unfinished Business: Pressure Points in the Lives of Women*. New York: Doubleday, 1980.

Seligman, Ph.D., Martin E. P. *Learned Optimism*. New York: Knopf, 1991.

Seligman, Ph.D., Martin E. P. "Three Smart Ways to Beat the Blues." *Ladies' Home Journal*, April 1994, pp. 56, 60.

Seligman, Ph.D., Martin E. P. *What You Can Change and What You Can't*. New York: Knopf, 1994.

Siegel, M.D., Bernie. *Peace, Love and Healing*. New York: Harper & Row, 1989.

Tan, Siang-Yang. "The ABCs of Depression." *Christian Counseling Today*. Fall 1995, pp. 10-13.

The Boston Women's Health Book Collective. *The New Our Bodies, Ourselves: A Book by and for Women*. New York: Simon & Schuster, 1992.

"The Right Treatments for Your Troubles." *Consumer Reports*, November 1995, p. 737.

Thompson, Tracy. "The Wizard of Prozac." *Reader's Digest*, October 1994, pp. 73-77. (Condensed from *Washington Post*, 21 November 1993.)

Thorne, Julia, with Larry Rothstein. *You Are Not Alone*. New York: Harper Collins, 1993.

Thurman, Chris. "Developing the Mind of Christ." *Christian Counseling Today*, Fall 1995, pp. 20-24.

Toufexis, Anastasia. "Dark Days, Darker Spirits." *Time*, 11 January 1988, p. 66.

Trent, John. "Bringing Hope to the Discouraged." *Christian Counseling Today*, Fall 1995, p. 59.

Turkington, Carol, and Eliot F. Kaplan, M.D. *Making the Prozac Decision*. Los Angeles, Calif.: Lowell House, 1994.

U.S. Department of Health and Human Services Public Health Service. *A Consumer's Guide to Services Mental Health/Mental Illness*. 1992 edition.

Wallis, Claudia. "The Estrogen Dilemma." *Time*, 26 June 1995, pp. 46, 48-53.

Wartik, Nancy. "Defeating Depression." *American Health*, December 1993, pp. 39-41, 43-45, and 86.

Wright, H. Norman. *Questions Women Ask in Private*. Ventura, Calif.: Regal, 1993.

Zonis, Nadia. "The Healthy Way to Fight PMS." *Good Housekeeping*, August 1995, p. 149.

Notes

Chapter One: Knowing Makes All the Difference

1. Ellen McGrath, Ph.D., *When Feeling Bad Is Good* (New York: Henry Holt and Company, 1992), p. 4.
2. Martin E. P. Seligman, Ph.D., *Learned Optimism* (New York: Knopf, 1991), p. 64.
3. McGrath, p. 19.

Chapter Two: All Women Are Not Equal

1. Donald F. Klein and Paul H. Wender, *Understanding Depression: A Complete Guide to Its Diagnosis and Treatment* (New York: Oxford University Press, 1993), pp. 87-88.
2. Nancy Wartik, "Defeating Depression," *American Health*, December 1993, p. 43.
3. Sandra Salmans, *Depression* (Allentown, Penn.: People's Medical Society, 1995), p. 56.
4. Wartik, p. 43.
5. Carol Turkington with a foreword by Eliot F. Kaplan, M.D., *Making the Prozac Decision* (Los Angeles, Calif.: Lowell House, 1994), p. 31.
6. Susan Nolen-Hoeksema, *Sex Differences in Depression* (Stanford, Calif.: Stanford University Press, 1990), p. 44.
7. Klein and Wender, pp. 92-93.

Chapter Three: Recognizing the Clues

1. John H. Greist, M.D., and James W. Jefferson, M.D., *Depression and Its Treatment* (Washington, D.C.: American Psychiatric Press, 1992), p. 2.

Chapter Four: Unmasking the Faces of Depression

1. David D. Burns, M.D., *The Feeling Good Handbook* (New York: A Plume Book published by the Penguin Group, 1989) p. 57.
2. Criteria for major depression is included in almost all books on depression. This list is a paraphrase of the criteria listed by John H. Greist, M.D., and James W. Jefferson, M.D., *Depression and Its Treatment* (Washington, D.C.: American Psychiatric Press, 1992), pp. 30-31. Greist and Jefferson's list comes from the

Diagnostic and Statistical Manual of the American Psychiatric Association, 1987. Clinicians in the United States use the DSM criteria for making diagnoses.

3. Greist and Jefferson, *Depression and Its Treatment*, p. 30.
4. Greist and Jefferson, p. 32.
5. Martin E. P. Seligman, Ph.D., *What You Can Change and What You Can't* (New York: Knopf, 1994), p. 105.
6. Paraphrase of criteria listed in Greist and Jefferson, pp. 113-114.
7. Greist and Jefferson, p. 113.
8. Ellen McGrath, Ph.D., *When Feeling Bad Is Good* (New York: Henry Holt and Company, 1992), p. 287.
9. *Depression Is a Treatable Illness* (Rockville, Md.: U.S. Department of Health and Human Services, 1993), p. 8.
10. Greist and Jefferson, p. 129.
11. Julia Thorne with Larry Rothstein, *You Are Not Alone* (New York: Harper Collins, 1992), p. 129.
12. Anastasia Toufexis, "Dark Days, Darker Spirits," *Time*, 11 January 1988, p. 66.
13. Simeon Margolis, M.D., Ph.D., and Peter V. Rabins, M.D., M.P.H., *The Johns Hopkins White Papers on Depression and Anxiety* (Baltimore, Md.: The Johns Hopkins Medical Institutions, 1995), p. 10.
14. Burns, p. 57.
15. "Long-Term Blues," *American Health*, December 1993, p. 45.

Chapter Five: What Triggers Depression

1. Kenneth S. Kendler, M.D., Ronald C. Kessler, Ph.D., Michael C. Neale, Ph.D., Andrew C. Heath, D.Phil., and Lindon J. Eaves, Ph.D., D.Sc., "The Prediction of Major Depression in Women: Toward an Integrated Etiologic Model," *The American Journal of Psychiatry*, August 1993, pp. 1139-1148.
2. Susan Nolen-Hoeksema, *Sex Differences in Depression* (Stanford, Calif.: Stanford University Press, 1990), p. 68.
3. Archibald D. Hart, Ph.D., *Coping with Depression in the Ministry and Other Helping Professions* (Waco, Tex.: Word, 1984), p. 553.
4. Hart, p. 56.
5. Hart, p. 56.
6. LynNell Hancock with Debra Rosenberg, Karen Springen, Patricia King, Patrick Rogers, Martha Brant, Claudia Kalb, and T. Trent Gegax, "Breaking Point," *Newsweek*, 6 March 1995, p. 59.
7. Martin E. P. Seligman, Ph.D., *What You Can Change & What You Can't* (New York: Knopf, 1994), p. 109.
8. Seligman, "Three Smart Ways to Beat the Blues," *Ladies' Home Journal*, April 1994, p. 56.
9. Seligman, *What You Can Change and What You Can't*, p. 109.
10. Siang-Yang Tan, "The ABCs of Depression," *Christian Counseling Today*, Fall 1995, p. 12.
11. Ecclesiastes 1:2,14, NKJV.
12. Nolen-Hoeksema, p. 79.
13. David J. McKay, Ph.D., "Uncovering Emotion: Finding the Feelings Behind Depression," *Christian Counseling Today*, Fall 1995, p. 26.

Chapter Six: What's Your Body Telling You?

1. Ellen McGrath, Gwendolyn Puryear Keita, Bonnie R. Strickland, and Nancy Felipe Russo, *Women and Depression* (Washington, D.C.: American Psychological Association, 1990), p. 9.
2. Maggie Scarf, *Unfinished Business: Pressure Points in the Lives of Women* (Garden City, N.Y.: Doubleday, 1980), p. 285.
3. Colette Dowling, *You Mean I Don't Have to Feel This Way?* (New York: Scribner, 1991), pp. 84-85.
4. Dowling, p. 89.
5. Carol Turkington with a foreword by Eliot F. Kaplan, M.D., *Making the Prozac Decision* (Los Angeles, Calif.: Lowell House, 1994), p. 18.
6. Turkington and Kaplan, p. 18.
7. McGrath, Keita, Strickland, and Russo, p. 10.
8. Ruth Nemtzow, CSW, "Childbirth: Happiness, Blues, or Depression?" *Women and Depression: A Lifespan Perspective* (New York: Springer, 1987), p. 135.
9. Nemtzow, p. 135.
10. Scarf, p. 286.
11. Scarf, p. 286.
12. Scarf, p. 286.
13. Scarf, p. 286.
14. Scarf, p. 280.
15. Scarf, p. 279.
16. Dana Jack, "Silencing the Self: The Power of Social Imperatives in Female Depression," *Women and Depression: A Lifespan Perspective* (New York: Springer Publishing Company, 1987), p. 161.
17. Eileen Hoffman, M.D., *Our Health, Our Lives* (New York: Simon & Schuster, 1995), p. 251.
18. Dowling, p. 97.
19. Paula Dranov, "Tired? Depressed?" *Reader's Digest*, January 1995, p. 18.
20. Martin E.P. Seligman, Ph.D., *What You Can Change and What You Can't* (New York: Knopf, 1994), pp. 107-108.
21. McGrath, Keita, Strickland, and Russo, p. 10.

Chapter Seven: The People Connection

1. Maggie Scarf, *Unfinished Business: Pressure Points in the Lives of Women* (Garden City, N.Y.: Doubleday, 1980), p. 527.
2. Carol Gilligan, *In a Different Voice* (Cambridge, Mass.: Harvard University Press, 1982), p. 9.
3. Gilligan, p. 10.
4. Gilligan, p. 159.
5. Gilligan, p. 163.
6. Deborah Tannen, *You Just Don't Understand* (New York: Morrow, 1990), p. 77.
7. Ellen McGrath, Gwendolyn Puryear Keita, Bonnie R. Strickland, and Nancy Felipe Russo, *Women and Depression* (Washington, D.C.: American Psychological Association, 1990), p. 22.
8. Ruth Formanek and Anita Gurian, ed., *Women and Depression: A Lifespan Perspective* (New York: Springer, 1987), p. 34.

9. Scarf, p. 86.
10. Scarf, pp. 534-535.
11. McGrath, Keita, Strickland, and Russo, p. 22.
12. *Depression: What Every Woman Should Know* (Rockville, Md.: National Institutes of Health, Publication No. 95-3871), p. 7.
13. *Depression: What Every Woman Should Know*, p. 7.
14. Eileen Hoffman, M.D., *Our Health, Our Lives* (New York: Simon & Schuster, 1995), p. 276.
15. McGrath, Keita, Strickland, and Russo, p. 23.
16. Aaron T. Beck, M.D., "Why Husbands Won't Talk," *Reader's Digest*, December 1988, p. 13.
17. McGrath, Keita, Strickland, and Russo, p. 22.
18. Hoffman, p. 276.
19. McGrath, Keita, Strickland, and Russo, pp. 85-86.
20. McGrath, Keita, Strickland, and Russo, p. 23.
21. Formanek and Gurian, p. 289.
22. Dr. Joyce Brothers, "Men and Women—The Differences," *Woman's Day*, 9 February 1982, p. 142.
23. Brothers, p. 142.
24. McGrath, Keita, Strickland, and Russo, p. 23.
25. Hoffman, p. 276.
26. McGrath, Keita, Strickland, and Russo, p. 22.
27. An interview with Dr. Archibald Hart, "Understanding Depression," *Focus on the Family*, March 1993, p. 6.
28. McGrath, Keita, Strickland, and Russo, p. 86.
29. McGrath, Keita, Strickland, and Russo, p. 86.
30. Ellen McGrath, Ph.D., *When Feeling Bad Is Good* (New York: Henry Holt and Company, 1992).
31. Scarf, page 535.
32. McGrath, page 289.

Chapter Eight: The Cultural Connection

1. Marsha Lasswell and Thomas Lasswell, *Marriage and the Family* (Belmont, Calif.: Wadsworth, 1991), p. 37.
2. Dana Jack, "Silencing the Self: The Power of Social Imperatives in Female Expression," *Women and Depression: A Lifespan Perspective* (New York, N.Y.: Springer, 1987), p. 61.
3. Jack, p. 162.
4. Jack, p. 162.
5. Jack, p. 164.
6. Jack, p. 164.
7. Jack, p. 167.
8. Jack, p. 164.
9. Jack, p. 164.
10. Jack, p. 168.
11. Jack, p. 173.
12. Jack, p. 177.

13. Jack, p. 178.
14. Ellen McGrath, Ph.D., *When Feeling Bad Is Good* (New York: Henry Holt and Company, 1992), p. 53.
15. McGrath, p. 62.
16. McGrath, p. 224.
17. Martin E. P. Seligman, Ph.D., *What You Can Change and What You Can't* (New York: Knopf, 1994), p. 190.
18. Seligman, p. 190.
19. Jack, p. 177.
20. Seligman, p. 108.
21. Seligman, p. 108.

Chapter Nine: Responses to Trouble

1. Martin E. P. Seligman, Ph.D., *Learned Optimism* (New York: Knopf, 1991), p. 86.
2. Seligman, p. 86.
3. David Burns, M.D., *Feeling Good: The New Mood Therapy* (New York: The New American Library, 1980), p. 34.
4. Seligman, p. 46.
5. Burns, p. 39.
6. Aaron T. Beck, M.D., "Love Is Never Enough," *Reader's Digest*, April 1989, p. 58.

Chapter Ten: When the Roots Grow Deep

1. James C. Neely, M.D., *Gender, The Myth of Equality* (New York: Simon & Schuster, 1981), p. 111.
2. Maggie Scarf, *Unfinished Business: Pressure Points in the Lives of Women* (Garden City, N.Y.: Doubleday, 1980), pp. 432-433.
3. Erica E. Goode with Nancy Linnon and Sarah Burke, "Beating Depression," *U.S. News & World Report*, 5 March 1990, p. 55.
4. Ellen McGrath, Ph.D., *When Feeling Bad Is Good* (New York: Henry Holt and Company, 1992), p. 44.
5. McGrath, p. 39.
6. Frank B. Minirth and Paul D. Meier, *Happiness Is a Choice, A Manual on the Symptoms, Causes, and Cures of Depression* (Grand Rapids, Mich.: Baker, 1978), p. 47.
7. Goode, Linnon, and Burke, p. 55.
8. Martin E. P. Seligman, Ph.D., *What You Can Change and What You Can't* (New York: Knopf, 1994), p. 231.
9. Goode, Linnon, and Burke, p. 55.
10. Eileen Hoffman, M.D., *Our Health, Our Lives* (New York: Simon & Schuster, 1995), p. 278.
11. Hoffman, p. 292.
12. Collette Dowling, *You Mean I Don't Have to Feel This Way?* (New York: Scribner, 1991), p. 79.
13. Susan Nolen-Hoeksema, *Sex Differences in Depression* (Stanford, Calif.: Stanford University Press, 1990), p. 178.
14. Nolen-Hoeksema, p. 194.
15. Nancy Wartik, "Defeating Depression," *American Health*, December 1993, p. 43.

16. Nolen-Hoeksema, p. 194.
17. Hoffman, p. 292.
18. H. Norman Wright, *Questions Women Ask in Private* (Ventura, Calif.: Regal, 1993), p. 99.
19. Edie McCoy Meeks as told to Jane Marks, "Making Peace with the Past: One Woman's Story," *McCall's*, March 1994, p. 36.

Chapter Eleven: Do You Want to Get Well?
1. *Depression Is a Treatable Illness* (Rockville, Md.: U.S. Department of Health and Human Services, April 1993), p. 4.
2. Erica E. Goode with Nancy Linnon and Sarah Burke, "Beating Depression," *U.S. News & World Report*, 5 March 1990, p. 55.
3. Carl Rogers quoted by Bruce Larson, *There's a Lot More to Health Than Not Being Sick* (Waco, Tex.: Word, 1981), p. 47.

Chapter Twelve: Helping Yourself Through Action
1. Dr. David D. Burns, *Feeling Good, The New Mood Therapy* (New York: The New American Library, 1980), p. 92.
2. Burns, p. 92.
3. Susan Nolen-Hoeksema, *Sex Differences in Depression* (Stanford, Calif.: Stanford University Press, 1990), pp. 174-175.

Chapter Thirteen: Lord, I Need Your Help . . .
1. Mary Ellen Copeland, *Living Without Depression and Manic Depression* (Oakland, Calif.: New Harbinger Publications, 1994), pp. 186-187.

Chapter Fourteen: Do You Need Professional Help?
1. Archibald D. Hart, Ph.D., *Coping with Depression in the Ministry and Other Helping Professions* (Waco, Tex.: Word, 1984), p. 102.
2. *Depression Is a Treatable Illness* (Rockville, Md.: U.S. Department of Health and Human Services, April 1993), p. 24.
3. Carol Turkington with a foreword by Eliot F. Kaplan, M.D., *Making the Prozac Decision* (Los Angeles, Calif.: Lowell House, 1994), p. 14.
4. Turkington and Kaplan, pp. 14-15.
5. Turkington and Kaplan, p. 15.
6. Turkington and Kaplan, p. 14.
7. Turkington and Kaplan, p. 15.
8. Simeon Margolis, M.D., Ph.D, and Peter V. Rabins, M.D., M.P.H., *The Johns Hopkins White Papers on Depression and Anxiety* (Baltimore, Md.: The Johns Hopkins Medical Institutions, 1995), p. 23.
9. John H.Greist, M.D., and James W. Jefferson, M.D., *Depression and Its Treatment* (Washington, D.C.: American Psychiatric Press, 1992), p. 74.
10. Greist and Jefferson, p. 73.
11. Greist and Jefferson, p. 73.
12. Greist and Jefferson, p. 73.
13. Maggie Scarf, *Unfinished Business: Pressure Points in the Lives of Women* (Garden

City, N.Y.: Doubleday, 1980), p. 498.
14. Greist and Jefferson, p. 73.
15. Greist and Jefferson, p. 74.
16. "Who Knocks Shocks?" *Psychology Today*, November/December 1995, p. 14.
17. "Who Knocks Shocks?" *Psychology Today*, p. 14.
18. Margolis and Rabins, p. 24.
19. Sandra Salmans, *Depression* (Allentown, Penn.: People's Medical Society, 1995), p. 78.
20. *Helpful Facts about Depressive Illnesses* (Rockville, Md.: National Institute of Mental Health, 1989), p. 2.

Chapter Fifteen: Making Sense of Antidepressants
1. Carol Turkington with a foreword by Eliot F. Kaplan, M.D., *Making the Prozac Decision* (Los Angeles, Calif.: Lowell House, 1994), p. 99.
2. Turkington and Kaplan, pp. 99-100.
3. Turkington and Kaplan, pp. 121-122.
4. John H. Greist, M.D., and James W. Jefferson, M.D., *Depression and Its Treatment* (Washington, D.C.: American Psychiatric Press, Inc.), 1992, p. 65.
5. Sandra Salmans, *Depression* (Allentown, Penn.: People's Medical Society, 1995), p. 129.
6. Harold H. Bloomfield, M.D., and Peter McWilliams, *How to Heal Depression* (Los Angeles, Calif.: Prelude Press, 1994), p. 82.
7. Turkington and Kaplan, p. 91.
8. Claudia Bowe, "Women and Depression: Are We Being Overdosed?" *Redbook*, March 1992, p. 44.
9. Michael J. Norden, M.D., *Beyond Prozac* (New York: Harper Collins, 1995), p. 161.
10. Norden, p. 198.
11. Michael W. Miller, "A New Antidepressant Will Challenge Prozac," *Wall Street Journal*, 29 December 1993, p. B1.
12. Turkington and Kaplan, p. 151.
13. Greist and Jefferson, p. 69.
14. Martin E. P. Seligman, Ph.D., *What You Can Change and What You Can't* (New York: Knopf, 1993), p. 110.
15. Turkington and Kaplan, p. x.
16. Salmans, p. 121.
17. Turkington and Kaplan, p. 55.

Chapter Sixteen: Four Effective Therapies
1. Erica E. Goode, "For a Little Peace of Mind," *U.S. News & World Report*, 28 September 1987, p. 98.
2. Sandra Salmans, *Depression* (Allentown, Penn.: People's Medical Society, 1995), p. 89.
3. Jean Fain, "Depression Update," *Ladies' Home Journal*, January 1991, p. 60.
4. Ellen McGrath, Ph.D., *When Feeling Bad Is Good* (New York: Henry Holt and Company, 1992), p. 292.
5. McGrath, p. 292.

6. McGrath, p. 293.
7. Masculine pronouns will be used to refer to therapists. Even though therapists include both men and women, using masculine pronouns will simplify the reading. "He" will refer to the therapist, and "she" will refer to the patient or client.
8. Ellen McGrath, Gwendolyn Puryear Keita, Bonnie R. Strickland, and Nancy Felipe Russo, *Women and Depression* (Washington, D.C.: American Psychological Association, 1990), p. 58.
9. Salmans, p. 111.

Chapter Seventeen: Meeting the Difficulties Head-On

1. "In the Beginning," *U.S. News & World Report*, 28 September 1987, p. 98.
2. "Does Therapy Help?" *Consumer Reports*, November 1995, p. 739.
3. David D. Burns, M.D., *The Feeling Good Handbook* (New York: A Plume Book published by the Penguin Group, 1989), p. 504.
4. Burns, p. 505.
5. Burns, p. 505.
6. Brian O'Reilly, "Depressed? Here's Help," *Reader's Digest*, April 1994, p. 154.
7. Ellen McGrath, Gwendolyn Puryear Keita, Bonnie R. Strickland, and Nancy Felipe Russo, *Women and Depression* (Washington, D.C.: American Psychological Association, 1990), p. 91.
8. McGrath, Keita, Strickland, and Russo, pp. 91-92.
9. David D. Burns, M.D., *Feeling Good, The New Mood Therapy* (New York: The New American Library, 1980), p. 83.
10. O'Reilly, p. 157.
11. O'Reilly, p. 157.
12. Nancy Wartik, "Defeating Depression," *American Health*, December 1993, p. 44.
13. Julia Thorne with Larry Rothstein, *You Are Not Alone* (New York: Harper Collins, 1993), pp. 103-104.
14. Thorne and Rothstein, p. 103.
15. Thorne and Rothstein, p. 103.
16. Thorne and Rothstein, p. 104.
17. Carol Turkington and Eliot F. Kaplan, M.D., *Making the Prozac Decision* (Los Angeles, Calif.: Lowell House, 1994), p. x.
18. *Depression Is a Treatable Illness* (Rockville, Md.: U.S. Department of Health and Human Services, 1993), p. 15.

Chapter Eighteen: Getting the Support You Need

1. Dee Brestin's quote from *For My Friend: Thoughts of You Cheer My Heart* (Bloomington, Minn.: Garborg's, 1995).

Chapter Nineteen: Your Sense of Self

1. Quoted by Mary Wilder Tileston, *Joy & Strength* (Minneapolis, Minn.: World Wide, 1986), p. 242.
2. Joyce Brothers, *Positive Plus* (New York: Putnam, 1994), p. 71.
3. Brothers, p. 74.
4. Brothers, p. 82.

5. Arthur Ashe, "Personal Glimpses," *Reader's Digest*, April 1995, p. 34.
6. Brothers, p. 84.
7. Sue Shellenbarger, "Women Indicate Satisfaction with Role of Big Breadwinner," *Wall Street Journal*, 11 May 1995, p. B1.

Chapter Twenty-One: Building Spiritual Resistance
1. Mary Anne McManus, "Springtime Came Late," *Fullness Magazine*, January-February 1985, p. 4.
2. McManus, p. 5.
3. McManus, p. 5.
4. McManus, p. 5.
5. Dianne Hales, "Three Little Words That Will Heal You," *McCall's*, June 1994, pp. 102, 104, 106-107.
6. Bernie Siegel, M.D., *Peace, Love & Healing* (New York: Harper & Row, 1989), p. 219.
7. Siegel, p. 219.
8. Siegel, p. 219.

Chapter Twenty-Two: Ten Ways to Help Her Win
1. Collette Dowling, *You Mean I Don't Have to Feel This Way?* (New York: Scribner, 1991), p. 226.
2. Dowling, p. 227.
3. Dowling, p. 226.
4. Ellen McGrath, Gwendolyn Puryear Keita, Bonnie R. Strickland, and Nancy Felipe Russo, *Women and Depression* (Washington, D.C.: American Psychological Association, 1990), p. 56.

Epilogue
1. Hagar's story is in Genesis 16.
2. Susan Nolen-Hoeksema, *Sex Differences in Depression* (Stanford, Calif.: Stanford University Press, 1990), p. 214.

Author

BRENDA POINSETT met her husband, Bob, while they were both graduate students at Southwestern Baptist Theological Seminary in Fort Worth, Texas. Following their marriage, she used her theological education to write, speak, teach Sunday school, lead prayer groups, and enrich their family life. Her main interests were missions, prayer, and spiritual celebrations. She wrote curriculum material for the Women's Missionary Union of the Southern Baptist Convention and then two books on prayer: *Prayerfully Yours* and *When Jesus Prayed* (Broadman Press). She led workshops to help families put more of Christ in their Christmas celebrations. From this, she published *Celebrating the Life of Jesus*, a book of daily December devotions for families.

Her unexpected struggle with depression opened up new writing opportunities: *Understanding a Woman's Depression* (Tyndale, 1984), *I'm Glad I'm a Woman* (Tyndale, 1988), and *Why Do I Feel This Way?* (NavPress, 1996).

In 1985 Bob and Brenda—along with their three sons, Jim, Joel, and Ben—moved to Bedford, Indiana. Brenda began teaching on an adjunct basis at Oakland City University's branch campus. She teaches Old Testament Literature, New Testament Literature, Women of the Bible, and Marriage and the Family. A byproduct of her teaching was the publication of *Old Testament Survey: A Student's Guide* (Broadman and Holman).

To purchase Brenda's books or to contact her for speaking engagements, you may write to her at Oakland City University-Bedford, P.O. Box 455, Bedford, Indiana 47421.